IT'S TIME

VOICES FROM
THE FRONT LINES OF
URBAN MISSION

Mission to the Cities Committee,
General Conference of Seventh-day Adventists

Edited by Bettina Krause

ISBN 978-1-943507-02-3

Printed in the United States of America

Cover and Interior Text Designer: Ellen Musselman

CONTRIBUTORS

Paolo Benini, *director, Adventist Mission,*
Inter-European Division of Seventh-day Adventists

Nathan Brown, *book editor, Signs Publishing Company,*
South Pacific Division of Seventh-day Adventists

Fabrício Francisco de Fraga, *assistant pastor,*
Portão Seventh-day Adventist Church, Brazil

Kwon JohngHaeng, *director, Adventist Mission,*
Northern Asia-Pacific Division of Seventh-day Adventists

Bettina Krause, *communication director, Public Affairs and*
Religious Liberty department, General Conference of Seventh-day Adventists

Gary Krause, *director, Adventist Mission,*
General Conference of Seventh-day Adventists

Silas Gomes de Oliveira Neto, *senior pastor,*
Portão Seventh-day Adventist Church, Brazil

Catherine Nyameino, *communication director,*
East Kenya Union Conference of Seventh-day Adventists

Jerry Page, *secretary, Ministerial Association,*
General Conference of Seventh-day Adventists

Reylourd Reyes, *co-founder, Simply Missions, Manila, Philippines*

Michael L. Ryan, *general vice president,*
General Conference of Seventh-day Adventists

Gerson P. Santos, *director, Global Mission Urban Ministry Study Center,*
General Conference of Seventh-day Adventists

Wes Via, *past director, Simplicity Outreach Center, Pennsylvania, United States*

TABLE OF CONTENTS

PREFACE

MEETING THE CHALLENGE OF THE CITIES

The need is urgent. The time is now.

THERE ARE THREE HUGE REASONS WHY Seventh-day Adventists must urgently carry forward mission into the great urban centers of the world.

- **God said so.** Matthew 28:19, 20, does not leave any wiggle room. World events point to Jesus' soon return, time is short, and thereby mission to the cities becomes urgent and absolutely essential. Now.

- **More than a hundred years ago, Ellen White called the church to increase its efforts and focus on city work.** Imagine what she might say today. The ratio of Adventists to population is far lower in cities than in rural areas and islands. We can be thankful for what has been done in the past, but the church of this hour in history must not neglect the urban work that stands before it.

- **Cities are where the people live.** The majority of the world's population crowds the cities, and the percentage increases every day. The shifting population from rural to urban presents both a challenge and an opportunity.

"Mission to the Cities" is a world initiative that calls the church to develop a growth plan for every city in the world with a population greater than 1 million.[1] Planting new congregations must be central to that plan. There are 535 cities with a population greater than 1 million. Many of those cities are greater than 10 million, and an increasing number are larger than 25 million.

Mission to the cities may seem impossible. Yes, work in cities is diffi-

---

1 At a five-day urban mission conference held October 2013 at the General Conference in Silver Spring, Maryland, delegates voted a plan to emphasize urban outreach in every Division of the world field. The full text of this document is included in the appendix of this book.

cult. Church members are busy, with little time to engage in mission. The population is full of people whose lives are often defined by dollar bills or Hollywood. The cost of mission workers, housing, property, and operations is far higher in cities than urban areas. Great news—impossibilities do not exist with God.

We've witnessed the great slums of Dhaka, Bangladesh; watched rivers of refugees cross borders, doubling city populations in 60 days; seen the hollow eyes of mothers desperate to feed their babies; watched weeping, sad-faced, lonely people in upscale neighborhoods; stared as hopeless people slept beside raw stagnant sewage; and prayed with people living in a house made of sticks and United Nations flour sacks. The question shouted in our ears: "Where is Jesus' method?"

Why is this book being written on city mission?

Perhaps there might be one person who reads this book and will recognize the call of God. The church has been instructed to pursue city work and to develop simple methods that will draw people to see and know Jesus. We have been instructed to use Christ's method alone.

What was His method? He went where people were. He touched them in sympathy and compassion. He healed them. He called them to God's word. He appealed to them to forsake their sins, put on His robe of righteousness, and follow Him to the kingdom for eternity.

These methods are being implemented around the world in cities of every nation, kindred, tongue, and people. People who are involved in God's mission recognize that the world is hungry for hope. Poverty, loneliness, depression, sickness, and fear are rapidly becoming the status quo. This only states what everyone already knows. These conditions are all around us.

How does the church go forward in mission? Will the church ever be clever enough, smart enough, or rich enough to engineer the finishing of the work? Certainly not. The work will be finished by the power of the Holy Spirit working through people whose lives are experiencing spiritual revival and reformation. They will be people of the Word and people of prayer.

It's a miracle of the Holy Spirit that anyone becomes involved in mission. Every conversion is a miracle of the Holy Spirit. Planting a new congregation is a miracle of the Holy Spirit. God's purpose for cities will not be realized because of cleverly laid human plans.

This book contains stories of God's leading and providence. It's filled with real-life experiences describing how God's mission team is establishing the kingdom in the hearts of city people around the world.

These stories provide a small glimpse into the lives of people who have chosen to turn their world upside down and become involved in God's mission. They provide a small glimpse into the lives of people who have traded their rags for robes of righteousness. These stories provide beginning evidence that the march into the cities has begun and the call to service rings throughout the church. Will you be part of it?

Michael L. Ryan
Chairman, Mission to the Cities Committee
General Vice President, General Conference of Seventh-day Adventists

Jerry Page
Secretary, Mission to the Cities Committee
Secretary, Ministerial Association of the General Conference of
Seventh-day Adventists

INTRODUCTION

*Do we have a strategy for making
disciples in the cities? Is it working?*

GERSON P. SANTOS

I WAS STANDING AT THE CORNER OF LEXINGTON AVENUE and 59th Street in Manhattan, waiting for Justin. I'd met him a few weeks earlier at lunch after church service. He had been sitting at the other end of the table, and I hadn't had a chance to talk much with him. I needed to leave the lunch for another appointment, but, noticing he wanted to continue the conversation, I gave Justin my business card and invited him to contact me in two weeks when I returned from a trip. When he did, we made plans to meet in front of Bloomingdales. (I wouldn't meet someone there if I had my wife, Leila, with me—we would definitely be late for the appointment.)

After greeting each other, Justin and I walked a few blocks to the restaurant. Born in India, he had accepted Jesus as his Savior a few years earlier while still living there. In New York, between work and graduate studies, Justin had been "church shopping" for a while. He had developed friendships in several communities but was still looking for one to call home. We entered Yuva Frontier Indian Grill and found a quiet corner to sit. He asked what I wanted to eat, and I told him I needed a mild vegetarian meal. "No problem," said Justin, "they can do that; a lot of Americans visit this restaurant." He was correct. As I looked around, I noticed that the waiter and my new friend were the only Indians in the restaurant.

I've been thinking about that. Wouldn't it be a wonderful surprise to visit our churches and see more visitors than members? I guess that Indian restaurant has been very mission focused, successfully sharing Indian cuisine in the American society. From all reports, those Americans eating at the restaurant weren't just converts—many were repeat customers. They were Indian food disciples. In a way, this urban restaurant was doing a far better job than many Christian churches that only gather the saints together each weekend, with little concern about reaching out to their community.

As we look at the challenge of mission to the cities, we can't continue with business as usual. If we're serious about following God's call to the great urban areas of the world, then our focus must be outward rather than inward, and we must build disciples, not just conduct baptisms.

THE CALL TO MAKE DISCIPLES

"There are many Seventh-day Adventists who do not understand that to accept the cause of Christ means to accept His cross," writes Ellen White. "The only evidence they give in their lives of their discipleship is in the name they bear. But the true Christian regards his stewardship as a sacred thing. He perseveringly studies the Word, and yields up his life to the service of Christ."[1] Today many people—Christians and non-Christians—believe that you can be a Christian without being a disciple. In fact, little attention has been given to the main goal of the Great Commission, which is to "make disciples." Are we taking Jesus' words seriously? Do we have a disciple-making strategy for urban areas? If we do, is it working?

As we follow Christ's method in urban areas, our goal is to not only have people become church members but to have their lives transformed—to be disciples who make disciples. Ellen White says: "The object of the Christian life is fruit bearing—the reproduction of Christ's character in the believer that it may be reproduced in others."[2] It's not enough to use our outreach ministries as "bait" to attract people to church and then tell them something like, "Sit down, behave, and don't do anything wrong." We have a higher calling. What does discipleship mean in your church? What are you doing to help people mature in their relationship to Jesus?

It's easier to do what we call evangelism than it is to make disciples. You can give your personal testimony and lead someone to Christ in just a few minutes, but it takes years to make a disciple of someone. In reality, discipleship happens throughout our lifetime. We never really stop growing in our faith. Writes Ellen White, "When in conversion the sinner finds peace with God through the blood of the atonement, the Christian life has but just begun."[3]

Unfortunately, often we think of evangelism as a public event conducted by an expert whom we call an evangelist. The biblical view of evangelism is more than an event—it's a process, something that is ongoing. What if it could happen in urban offices, workshops, universities, schools, homes, and sporting clubs? What if it were happening every week? What if every church member were doing it in their own style, using the gifts God has given them? What if it were adapted to local culture? What if it were personal, real, and natural? The Great Commission was not, "Go and make converts," but rather, "Go and make disciples." In many ways we've done a great job at reaching

---

1 *Reflecting Christ*, 287.

2 *Christ's Object Lessons*, 67.

3 *The Faith I Live By*, 117.

lost people, but perhaps we're not doing so well in the area of discipleship—facilitating the process of maturing in Christ.

CHRIST'S METHOD ALONE

Building loving relationships is an essential part of any mission work in urban areas. In the beginning, the first man and woman started out in a perfect relationship with God (Gen. 1:27, 28). Sin broke that relationship, but Jesus came to heal and restore—and that restoration will be completed at the end of this world's history (Rev. 21:22). Ministry is joining with God in the work of healing all these areas of brokenness. We need to learn from Christ how to apply a healing touch to broken people. "Christ's method alone will give true success in reaching the people. The Savior mingled with men as one who desired their good. He showed His sympathy for them, ministered to their needs, and won their confidence. Then He bade them, 'Follow Me.' "[4]

This comprehensive approach to outreach is not only based upon a specific formula, but it also accords with several statements where Ellen White says that evangelism is not merely the proclamation of a message. She says, for example, "Preaching is a small part of the work to be done for the salvation of souls."[5] We need to live the gospel in a practical way. "The world will be convinced, not by what the pulpit teaches, but by what the church lives," she adds. "The minister in the desk announces the theory of the gospel; the practical piety of the church demonstrates its power."[6] Again: "The cities are to be worked, not merely preached to."[7] The effectiveness of any outreach initiative has to be understood within the paradigm of Christ's method, which is person oriented rather than production oriented.

DISCIPLESHIP AND URBAN MISSION

The mission field has moved to the city, and we as Adventists need to respond to this opportunity. The Bible tells us that human history started in a garden but assures us it will finish in a city. More than a hundred years ago, Ellen White wrote: "The work in the cities is essential work for this time. When the cities are worked as God would have them, the result will be the setting in operation of a mighty movement such as we have not yet witnessed."[8]

Today's global population is more than four times larger than when Mrs. White wrote these words, and the global urban population is 13 times greater. Should we not also be concerned?

---

4 *The Ministry of Healing*, 143.

5 *Christian Service*, 68.

6 Ibid., 67.

7 *Ministry to the Cities*, 95.

8 *Medical Ministry*, 304.

A recent Harvard study shows how urban culture transcends borders. Marlene Towns writes of the challenge anti-Western sentiment poses to businesses and other organizations wanting to work in certain areas of the world—particularly the Middle East and parts of Asia. She points out that many young adults in these regions closely identify with American urban youth culture—the world of hip-hop and rap music. According to her research, among Chinese undergraduates, this familiarity and identification "may mitigate hostility" toward America, and may actually make them more willing to buy American products. She calls this "good news for companies interested in extending their global reach."[9]

Although we as the Seventh-day Adventist Church are focused on extending our global reach, and our church was birthed in the United States, we are not selling an American product. However, the message is clear: world population may be growing exponentially, but in a sense the world has shrunk. Information today spreads at the speed of light. And as this gospel of the kingdom is preached and demonstrated in urban areas, we will increasingly see it transcending borders and cultural barriers. The urban environment brings people together not only in physical space but also through the connections of social and other media. The harvest is ripe.

THE CHALLENGE OF URBAN MISSION

As we look to the large cities of the world today we realize the complexity and diversity of these urban centers. "Most of the traditional ways of implementing Christian mission will not work effectively in the urban context."[10] Small-group ministries and church planting are extremely effective to make disciples and to fulfill God's mission. Especially in the cities, they give opportunity for creativity, innovation, and adaptability that are indispensable to reaching out to a diverse community. "Churches are to be planted," writes Ellen White. "No great centers are to be established, as at Battle Creek; and yet there will be some important churches raised up, and meeting-houses provided in large cities, favorable to accommodating the believers in [that locality]. There should not be a call to have settled pastors over our churches, but let the life-giving power of the truth impress the individual members to act, leading them to labor interestedly to carry on efficient missionary work in each locality."[11] The Bible doesn't describe the church as a building. It always refers to the church as a people—God's people, in Christ—sent by the Spirit to live a life of complete surrender to His service.

When Ellen White presented the challenge of the cities, she mentioned the need to "establish new centers of influence wherever an opening can be found. Rally workers

---

9   Marlene Morris Towns, "How Urban Culture Transcends Borders," *Harvard Business Review*, March 2014.

10   Monte Sahlin, *Mission in Metropolis: The Adventist Movement in the Urban World* (Lincoln, NE: Center for Creative Ministry, 2007), 3.

11   *AU Gleaner*, January 8, 1902.

who possess true missionary zeal, and let them go forth to diffuse light and knowledge far and near."[12] These centers connect the church to the community. They can feature a wide variety of activities such as lifestyle education, treatment rooms, bookstores, reading rooms, restaurants, literature ministry, lectures, small groups, instruction on preparing wholesome food, and much more. The activities of each center will vary, depending on an accurate assessment of local community needs.

The General Conference is working to revitalize Ellen White's concept of Centers of Influence and to establish a network of self-sustaining Life Hope Centers in key urban areas around the world. Life Hope Centers are an integrated evangelistic outreach. They provide an opportunity for everyone to be involved in ministry using their unique gifts.

THE GREAT COMMISSION IS OUR MISSION

A few months ago, while waiting at an airport for my next flight, I spoke on the phone to my wife, Leila. "It's snowing again," she said, "and you're not home to shovel the driveway." It feels good to me to be missed after a few days away from home! It was an unusual winter in New York, with record levels of snow, defying the long-range weather forecasters. Of course, it's hard to accurately predict snowfall several months in advance. For the past 10 years, 60 percent of one weather company's forecasts for seasonal snowfall were inaccurate.

But I have an explanation. I credit the snow to Fusion. Fusion is a new Adventist church plant in the Bronx, a borough in north New York City. Before they celebrated their first anniversary, the members were already operating several ministries in the community. One of them was a snow ministry. They would pray for snow and then go into the neighborhood with shovels to clean up sidewalks and driveways. When people asked them why they were doing this, they answered, "Because Jesus loves you, and so do we." No wonder we had so much snow last winter! This year I've already told them, "Please find another kind of ministry and pray for something else."

But we need more Fusions—missions to urban communities. Going in mission is not an optional extra—not just an upgrade for the "mature disciple." Going in mission is fundamental to the journey of discipleship. As soon as we start following Jesus, we should view ourselves as missionaries. As Ellen White wrote, "Every true disciple is born into the kingdom of God as a missionary."[13]

In working for the urban community, the church doesn't lose its identity, it strengthens it.

Leila has been very dedicated as a multi-grade teacher, trying to keep high academic standards and also to establish an environment to facilitate discipleship in her classroom. One day, Sammy, one of her fifth-graders, came to her and said, "Let me tell you about

---

12 *Testimonies for the Church*, 9:118.

13 *Christian Service*, 9.

my ministry." It's rewarding to see how real disciples can integrate in their daily lives kingdom principles and turn their lives into full-time ministry.

Christ gave His commission to His disciples (Matthew 28), and then, just before His ascension, He told them they would be His witnesses to Jerusalem, Judea, Samaria, and to the uttermost parts of the globe (Acts 1:8). They were to go everywhere, but the work wasn't to stop with them. "The Saviour's commission to the disciples included all the believers," writes Ellen White. "It includes all believers in Christ to the end of time."[14] She says that the command to go into all the world should not be lost sight of.

> We are called upon to lift our eyes to the "regions beyond." Christ tears away the wall of partition, the dividing prejudice of nationality, and teaches a love for all the human family. He lifts men from the narrow circle which their selfishness prescribes; He abolishes all territorial lines and artificial distinctions of society. He makes no difference between neighbors and strangers, friends and enemies. He teaches us to look upon every needy soul as our brother, and the world as our field.[15]

One morning as Leila and I were having breakfast, our granddaughter Sophia called us on FaceTime, which allows us to see each other as we talk on our cell phones. The first thing she did was put her index finger before her pink bright lips and whisper, "They're still sleeping, don't be loud." After a quick chat, she stood up from her bed. "I'm gonna have breakfast also!" she called and ran to the kitchen. Milk, apple puree, cereal. And then she said, "Grandma, you should have this cereal, it's really good. It's magic, the milk turns pink." Then she explained, "There are some little strawberry pieces that make the milk pink."

I want our churches to be "magical" like that. Some ordinary Christians get involved with new Christians. Following Jesus' methods, the Holy Spirit blends them all together, disciples and visitors flourish, they become like Jesus, and they impact their cities. It should be like that. It can be real, not magical.

---

14 *The Desire of Ages*, 821.

15 Ibid., 823.

CENTERS OF INFLUENCE: "SINGING THE LORD'S SONG" IN THE CITIES

BY GARY KRAUSE

Today's urban missionaries are rediscovering the power of Christ's incarnational method of reaching people.

T he year he turned 68, senior Adventist pioneer Elder Stephen Haskell and his wife, Hetty, went to the mission field. Not Asia. Not Africa. Not South America. They went to the heart of New York City. After living almost all their lives in the country, the Haskells moved into an apartment just a couple of blocks from the southwest corner of Central Park. Haskell marveled at the metropolis they now called home. "In this city there are some buildings over thirty stories high," he wrote. "In the building where we live there are fifty-three families. The building is seven stories high, and two elevators run night and day."[1]

The Haskells had moved into a landmark apartment building, the Windemere, in a neighborhood known as Hell's Kitchen. The apartment complex was built to help accommodate the rapidly growing middle class of the 1890s. It was noted for its cutting-edge technology, such as the telephone and hydraulic elevator.[2] But Elder Haskell feared they might be forgotten in this urban jungle. "Do not let our breth-ren forget to pray for us," he wrote in the *Advent Review and Sabbath Herald*. "Do not forget the address. It is 400 West 57th St., New York City. "[3]

Haskell was discovering that urban areas can be a dislocating experience. While surrounded by millions of people, you can still feel lost and alone. Easily forgotten. It was an experience familiar to the Jewish exiles to Babylon thousands of years earlier. They felt alienated—physically, emotionally, spiritually. They lamented their lost homeland and cried out, "How shall we sing the LORD's song in a strange land?" (Psalm 137:4, KJV).

This is a missiological question that echoes through the centuries. How do we sing our Lord's song in the strange territory of the city, where many of us don't naturally feel at home? How do we even begin an Adventist witness in megalopolises that loom like threatening Goliaths over the mission landscape?

---

1   Stephen Haskell, "The Bible Training School," *Advent Review and Sabbath Herald*, November 12, 1901, 739.

2   Jennifer Lee, "New Owner to Repair a Once-Grand Landmark," *New York Times*, May 21, 2009, http://cityroom.blogs.nytimes.com/2009/05/21/new-owner-tol-repair-a-once-grand-landmark/?_r=0.

3   *Advent Review and Sabbath Herald*, July 9, 1901, 448.

One thing is certain. We don't have the luxury of just sitting around thinking about the question. In 1909, more than a hundred years ago, Ellen White wrote: "We are far behind in doing the work that should have been done in these long-neglected cities."[4] Today the world's urban population is 13 times greater than when she was writing.

How did Mrs. White suggest we sing the Lord's song in the cities? She had a vision for establishing ministry centers in every city around the globe. She called them "small plants," "Christian missions," and "centers of influence."[5] These urban centers would serve as platforms for church members to follow Christ's method of ministry—mingling, showing sympathy, ministering to needs, winning confidence, and bidding people to follow Him.[6]

God basically told the Jewish exiles in Babylon to forget about going home. He told them to settle down, build houses, plant gardens, marry, and seek the *shalom* of the city. "But seek the welfare [*shalom*] of the city where I have sent you into exile, and pray to the Lord on its behalf, for its welfare [*shalom*] and you will find your welfare [*shalom*]" (Jer. 29:7, ESV). *Shalom* is a rich Hebrew word for blessing, peace, prosperity, welfare. And God was giving them an urban mission—to bless Babylon. Their task was to work and pray for its shalom.

Centuries later, Jesus worked for the *shalom* of the towns and villages where He ministered. And today, in following His method of ministry, we can also be a blessing to the cities. In fact, according to Ellen White, this is the only method that will bring true success in ministry. As we follow Christ's incarnational ministry in the cities, we will "rejoice with those who rejoice" and "weep with those who weep" (Rom. 12:15, ESV). We will relieve the poor, care for the sick, comfort the sorrowing and bereaved, teach the uneducated, and counsel the inexperienced. "Accompanied by the power of persuasion, the power of prayer, the power of the love of God," says Mrs. White, "this work will not, cannot, be without fruit."[7]

Ellen White commended the church in San Francisco for putting this method into practice. Just a handful of believers, they followed Jesus' example and worked for the shalom of the city. They operated a vegetarian café, a small school, and a "working men's" home. They ran treatment rooms, classes on healthful living, and homes for orphans. They nursed the sick, helped people find jobs, distributed literature. They visited people's homes, held public meetings, and, as though they weren't busy enough, also operated a ministry to sailors on the San Fran-

---

4 *Ministry to the Cities*, 26.

5 Ibid., 49, 145.

6 See *The Ministry of Healing*, 143.

7 *The Ministry of Healing*, 144.

cisco waterfront. No wonder Mrs. White dubbed this wholistic ministry a "bee-hive"—a place of nonstop activity for the kingdom. It was a model she longed to see repeated in every city.

Urban ministry beehives can be emotionally and physically taxing. So, not surprisingly, Ellen White also recommended establishing what she called "outpost centers" in rural locations, where those involved in urban mission could retire to be spiritually and physically refreshed and revived. These rural centers could also be used to bring other urban-dwellers to experience physical and spiritual renewal.

When Ellen White wrote of "centers of influence," she had in mind things such as vegetarian restaurants, reading rooms, lifestyle education classrooms, and treatment rooms. In a sense, it doesn't matter what the service and ministries are, as long as they are connecting to human need with the goal of showing God's love in practical ways, and introducing people to the Savior. Centers of Influence are launching pads to start new groups of believers.

Today around the world we see hundreds of different kinds of urban Centers of Influence being established. They include vegetarian restaurants and cafés, immigrant centers, music studios, counseling centers, health food stores, second-hand shops, and "English as a second language" schools. They may look different in different places, but they share a common purpose—to put Christ's method of ministry into practice and lead people to Jesus.

To learn more about urban Centers of Influence,
visit www.urbancenters.org and www.MissiontotheCities.org.

JESUS MINGLING

"THE SAVIOR *MINGLED* WITH MEN AS ONE WHO DESIRED THEIR GOOD."

ELLEN G. WHITE

"IN CHRISTCHURCH, NEW ZEALAND, AND NOW IN NEWCASTLE, AUSTRALIA, we have held neighborhood barbecues. With a lot of prayer—for God's favor, for His Spirit to open hearts, and for courage—I knock on doors inviting people. I tell them not to bring anything as friends from church are helping put on the meal.

"The idea is to be friendly. The 'churchiest' thing that happens is that I say grace and ask a blessing for our street and city. Other than that, it's up to people to mix, mingle, and be friendly.

"The first time we did it in Christchurch, we had 60 from church and 100 people from the neighborhood attend. This led to three people coming regularly to church, a small-group Bible study starting in one of the homes on our street, and several attending other community programs. At our new house here in Australia, we had 60 from church come to put on the meal and 31 neighbors. So far, six people have come to church, and two have asked for Bible studies."

Benjamin Rea *has served as an urban church planter and currently pastors the Wallsend Seventh-day Adventist Church in the city of Newcastle, Australia.*

"JESUS LEFT CLEAR ORIENTATION TO ALL WHO WOULD ONE DAY FOLLOW HIM: 'You are the salt of the earth' [Matt. 5:13, NIV]. But how does salt fulfill its purposes in any meal? It needs to be put in the cooking pan, and it has to be mixed in the food. Salt does nothing if it's kept inside the saltshaker. In the same way, if we want to be a positive influence in the community we seek to reach with God's love, we have to intentionally place ourselves in the 'cooking pan' and 'mix' ourselves with people around us. Anything will work, as long as we make them thirsty for the Living Water [John 4:10]. Be the flavor for Jesus!"

Kleber Gonçalves *is senior pastor of the Nova Semente Seventh-day Adventist Church in the heart of São Paulo, Brazil. He is also director of the Global Mission Center for Secular and Postmodern Studies.*

CHAPTER 1

CHURCHES BORN OF PRAYER

*Conventional wisdom said the church
couldn't grow, but God had other ideas.*

PAOLO BENINI

*I*N A PROSPEROUS, PROFOUNDLY SECULAR ITALIAN CITY, *a shrinking
Seventh-day Adventist church refused to bow to a future of slow decline. Instead of simply
trying to survive, it stepped out in faith with an ambitious prayer-based plan for growth.
The result? A revived mother church in one of the richest urban areas in the country has given
birth to three groups of new believers through focus on prayer, mission, and discipleship.*

BERGAMO, ITALY

The ratio of Seventh-day Adventists to the general population is lower in Italy than
in many 10/40 Window[16] countries. It's lower than secular Scandinavian countries.
It's even lower than what some consider the most secular country in Europe—the
Czech Republic. After more than 150 years of work in Italy, the number of members
is fewer than ten thousand.

And yet in one of the most beautiful cities in Italy, a place of prosperity and economic growth, the Adventist Church has been multiplying in size in recent years.
Tourists flock to the culturally rich, ancient city of Bergamo, an hour's drive from
the city of Milan in northern Italy's Lombardy region. And in this urban area, an
Adventist church grew in just seven years from 73 to 211 members. From an attendance of fewer than 60, it multiplied to three hundred. From a church struggling to
survive, it transformed into a mission-focused church-planting community.

---

16 The 10/40 Window is an area of the world encompassed by the 10th and 40th parallels
north of the equator. It is an area of significance to Christians because most of the countries within that area have few Christian adherents and have governments opposed to the
presence of Christianity.

These numbers may not seem significant by, say, African or South and Central American standards. But in the context of secular western Europe, they stand out as a tribute to God's power in the lives of a community of believers that earnestly prayed for His leading.

PRAYER PLUS ACTION

In 2006 a church member named Giuseppe moved from Sicily in the south of Italy to Bergamo. What he found in the spiritual and mission condition of the church concerned him. So he started to pray that God would help him find fellow church members who would join him in a process of spiritual revival and rededication to God. After some six months of intercessory prayer, Giuseppe started visiting some of the people on his prayer list. By the end of 2006, a small group of five people were holding regular prayer meetings as they sought God's guidance for what they should do for His kingdom.

At the same time, the Bergamo church began developing a leadership process with a new team of elders. They organized the church into small groups, and these Sabbath School "action units" became the supporting framework for church, pastoral, spiritual, and missionary activities. Soon, each Sabbath School action unit had appointed a leader and was engaging in weekly family small groups. Seventy percent of the members participated in these groups during the week and then met in Sabbath School to share experiences of the past week and for intercessory prayer.

The following year, the church set a specific goal: each family group, supported by the Sabbath School units, would become a church plant—a new community of believers. Three elders with their spouses became the first to put this vision into action.

The results were startling for a community of believers that had long experienced church decline rather than church growth. In 2009, a group began in Boario, a city in the Camonica Valley with more than 30,000 people, and by 2015 it had grown to 33 members, with more than 50 attending. A second group started the same year in Olgiate-Merate, a region of more than 50,000 people, and has since grown to 25 members with 55 attending. In 2011, a third group started in Treviglio-Caravaggio and has grown to 34 church members, with some 70 people attending.

Each one of these numbers represents men and women who have found new life in Christ and a place within His body of believers. Their stories give a glimpse into the different ways the Holy Spirit is using the praying members of Bergamo church to witness in this most difficult urban mission territory.

SONYA'S STORY: PRAYED INTO CHURCH

On a Sabbath morning in the autumn of 2007, after the worship service in Bergamo church, a young woman from Bolivia asked to meet with the pastor. Sonya introduced herself and told him the reason why she was attending church for the first time. The previous Wednesday she was traveling on a bus, praying to God and asking

BUILDING DISCIPLES

One principle drives all the programs and activities of Bergamo church. The growing community exists to train new believers to become disciple-makers. Eleven church members who are still young in the faith are helping give Bible studies to 15 new people. They are receiving practical training on how to give Bible studies, following Paul's advice to Timothy: "You therefore, my son, be strong in the grace that is in Christ Jesus. And the things that you have heard from me among many witnesses, commit these to faithful men who will be able to teach others also" (2 Timothy 2:1, 2, HCSB).

A person receiving Bible studies from a pastor or official Bible worker will understand the beauty of the biblical message but may get the idea that you have to be a pastor or Bible specialist to give Bible studies. This is why it is so important to train new believers, right from the start, to become disciple-makers.

This can be seen in the experience of Savino, who worked in the same factory with Bergamo church elder Paolo. They became friends and started studying the Bible together after work. Savino decided to become an Adventist, and two months before his baptism he began studying the Bible with a friend he met at the gym. He also leads a midweek family group, but because his wife is not yet ready for them to meet in their home, he meets his friends in his car parked outside. Savino has a list of people for whom he is praying, including his wife and their elder son.

what church He would like her to attend. During her prayer, a tall man approached and gently touched her on her shoulder.

"You are praying!" he said.

"Yes," she replied.

"If you want to go to a church," he said, "look for the Seventh-day Adventist church."

Sonya continued to pray but soon realized her prayer had been answered. "Today I'm here because of that," Sonya told the pastor. After Bible studies, Sonya was baptized. However, a few months later she stood at the front of the church and said goodbye to the church. "I'm going back to my home village," she announced, "because there is no Adventist church there."

Some time later the church heard from Sonya that her mother, her brother who had been in prison, and other relatives and neighbors had accepted Jesus Christ and now belonged to the Adventist family.

A Sabbath School action unit of the Bergamo church had placed Sonya on a prayer list long before she attended for the first time that autumn Sabbath morning. In fact, she lived in the same building as one of the Bergamo's church elders who was engaged in prayer ministry, and he had been specifically praying for her as his neighbor.

PRIMO'S STORY: FROM PRAYER LIST TO BAPTISM

Primo was 71 years old, and for 29 years he had been the general leader of the sales office of the Vatican printing house in northern Italy. His son, daughter-in-law, and grandchildren, who were members of the Bergamo church, were praying for him. When the church organized the Sabbath School action units, his name was on the prayer list of one of them. Every Sabbath, people prayed for Primo. One Sabbath the children ran a special program during the worship service, and Primo's grandchildren invited him to attend.

Just before the sermon began, the personal ministries leader shared the list of names for whom the church was praying. Primo, visiting an Adventist church for the first time, looked at the screen and saw his name on the prayer list. Rather than being upset, he was touched to know that a community was praying for him. He decided to study the Bible, and on the last Sabbath of the year his son Roberto, one of the church elders, baptized his father. The day of his baptism, Primo testified that for 29 years he had sold Bibles and religious books. "Even so, I never read the Word of God," he said. "Now I'm studying, reading, and meditating from the Bible. And today I'm here to become part of the family of God through baptism."

JUDITH'S STORY: FROM BROKEN LIFE TO BUILDING LIVES

One Sabbath evening, Judith, a young woman from Ecuador, entered the almost empty Bergamo church. Judith had been raised an Adventist but for 10 years had jumped from one broken relationship to another, fought loneliness, and attempted suicide more than once. She had reached rock bottom again, and that Sabbath morning, fighting against herself, she decided to look for an Adventist church. An Internet search showed the Bergamo church as the closest to where she lived.

Entering the church, she was warmly welcomed by some members, and they offered to visit her at home the following week. Paolo, a church elder and leader of a Sabbath School action unit, asked his group to pray for Judith. That week, he and his wife, Franca, visited Judith in Merate, a town 30 kilometers (18 miles) from Bergamo. It is a very developed, rich area with a high-density population and many factories and businesses. Judith asked to re-study the Bible, and they made an appointment to meet every Wednesday night. On the first Wednesday, to Paolo and Franca's surprise, some 15 people—some immigrants from South America and some Italians—were waiting for them. Soon a family group was begun.

WHEN HOME BECOMES CHURCH

The number of people attending Bible studies in Judith's house increased week after week. Soon a second family group was planted in the nearby town of Olgiate. At the beginning of 2012, the first baptisms took place, and soon they began Sabbath worship services. The following year, the group was officially organized with 14 members and 10 more attending. It became an official Global Mission project with the clear goal to plant a new church. Today there are 25 church members, 15 people studying the Bible and ready for baptism, plus friends and children. More than 50 people now attend each Sabbath.

This new group of believers continues as an extremely community-focused group, with a wholistic approach to mission. Every Wednesday morning they arrange a booth in the local marketplace, where they distribute Bibles and Bible correspondence cards. Every week, three family groups meet to study the Bible, and they invite friends and neighbors to join them. In each home they create a sense of fellowship in a loving, spiritual environment. On Friday evenings the children organize a special meeting for children and adults, followed by a meal together. The group is also training people to run health expo programs. Every Sabbath afternoon they hold two baptismal classes—one for beginners and another for advanced students—plus a special class on the books of Daniel and Revelation. They also hold public programs on building healthy families, educating children, healthy living, and how to know Jesus.

Sabbath morning before the program begins at 9:00, church members and their guests have breakfast together. The worship service is followed by potluck and fellowship, to which friends from the community are also invited. Sundays they often go hiking and have a picnic together in the countryside. At such times, the group often grows to 80 people. It's a terrific opportunity to make new friends.

A CHURCH THAT REFUSED TO STAGNATE

Lessons from the front lines of urban mission.

- **Focus on discipleship.** Baptism is only the beginning of the Christian experience. New believers should be trained immediately in how to become disciple-makers, not just members of a church.
- The experience of the Bergamo church raises the question, **"Why can't every house of a believer become a church?"** For the countries of secular Europe, this may be a model suited to outreach in urban environments.
- **Bathe everything in prayer.** Prayer started the Bergamo experience and continues to sustain its growth.

CHAPTER 2

HANGING OUT WITH PEOPLE, LIKE JESUS DID

Re-defining evangelism, one café meet-up at a time.

BETTINA KRAUSE[1]

*M*ETRO MANILA IS A BEHEMOTH OF A CITY; *actually, it's a cluster of 16 cities that's home to some 12 million people from every imaginable walk of life. But in this mass of humanity, a young Seventh-day Adventist pastor set his sights on making meaningful connections with one very specific group. In the process, he's finding new and creative ways of being an urban missionary.*

MAKATI, MANILA, PHILIPPINES

To the casual observer, it's just a regular evening scene at one of the many chic cafés in the upscale district of Makati, the financial heart of Metro Manila. The avenues outside are lined with high-end stores and towering office buildings. Inside the café there are the sounds of chairs scraping on the floor, the chatter of many different conversations blending with bursts of laughter from groups of young people seated around tables or lounging on comfortable sofas.

These are some of Manila's growing ranks of young, educated, upwardly mobile professionals. In a country where the average income is modest at best, this group of relatively high-income earners accounts for just 7 percent of the workforce yet is responsible for some 20 percent of the nation's spending on luxury items such as recreation and vacations.

If you look closer around the café you'll notice one group, seated at a long table near the rear of the café, that is particularly absorbed in conversation. The young people are talking and laughing, yet their conversation seems more focused, more intent than that of other groups in the room. Along with half-empty mugs and plates of food are small booklets—discussion guides called *CAFÉ Life* group module. Depending on

---

1   Thanks to E. Douglas Venn, Adventist Mission director for the Southern Asia-Pacific Division of Seventh-day Adventists, who gave invaluable assistance with this chapter.

the evening, the topic could be family, work life, finding love, emotional health, or building a healthy lifestyle.

This is a CAFÉ Life meet-up, one of many facilitated by Seventh-day Adventist young people each week around Metro Manila. These small-group meetings happen in public places—cafés or restaurants—and they have just one purpose: to connect secular young professionals with their Creator.

NOT A PROGRAM—AN IDEA

CAFÉ Life belongs to an umbrella ministry called Simply Missions—an urban ministry that's almost impossible to describe in just a few words. Its niche focus is young, secular, urban professionals in Manila, but the approach it takes doesn't fall neatly into any one urban ministry box.

Is it about evangelism training? Not specifically, but one of its outcomes is Adventist young people who are empowered to share their faith. Is it a small-group ministry? In one sense it is, but its scope is much broader. Is it a discipleship program? Yes, but that's not all. Is it a healthy-living ministry? Yes, in part, but that's just one piece of the puzzle.

The co-founder of Simply Missions, Pastor Reylourd Reyes, describes this urban ministry not as a project or program but as "an idea," which is the tagline that appears on the Simply Missions Web site and Facebook page.

"The idea of Simply Missions is not about classes, workshops, or training modules," says Reylourd. "It's not about becoming a missionary or an evangelist. It is about projecting the context of Jesus' mission, attitude, agenda, and mindset into our lifestyles."

Describing Simply Missions as an "idea" may sound somewhat vague, but it's an idea that has yielded some undeniably concrete results in the past four years. From just one group of friends meeting regularly in a café, Simply Missions has grown into what could be described as a "mission conglomerate": a whole range of interrelated ministries that aim to reach young professionals in Metro Manila. There are the CAFÉ Life evenings, which in many ways continue to be the backbone of Simply Missions. In recent times, this has branched out to include Internet meet-ups known as CAFÉ Life Online, and larger events called CAFÉ Life Next Level.

Then there's the higher level of connection called Project Grow, where regulars at the CAFÉ Life meetings are invited to more in-depth discussions, which introduce biblical principles. For many, this marks the beginning of a journey of spiritual growth and discipleship as part of a loving, supportive community. They attend Sabbath morning "Grow Gatherings," which Reylourd describes as seeker-sensitive worship services for yuppies (young urban professionals). They also become members of so-called Grow Groups, small groups that provide a strong, safe spiritual support group in which secular people can learn more about their Savior and His Word.

Another somewhat surprising aspect of Simply Mission is its travel arm, which organizes regular weekend road trips and getaways known as EPIC Weekends. These

PEOPLE, NOT PROJECTS

On his personal Web site, "Simply Pastor" (www.simplypastor.com/blog), Reylourd Reyes posts an eclectic collection of sermons, ideas, and random reflections. In one blog post, entitled, "They Are Not Projects," Reylourd considers the attitude we bring to urban ministry:

If you want to really annoy someone or tick them off, let them know they're a project you're trying to fix. Many of us are focused on trying to "fix" people rather than loving them right where they are. I've made many mistakes in the past trying to "fix" people. I'm sure I came off as judgmental, holier than thou, looking like I had an agenda, controlling, or simply an idiot.

How do you feel when you're "targeted"?

People are not projects.

But our motives are good, right? We want people to change for the better, we want them to get out of an unhealthy relationship, we want them to know Jesus, go to church, stop eating pork, get help for their marriage, stop abusing alcohol, and on and on . . . Often we have great motives but wrong methods.

Love is a choice; it's intentional. Think intentional relationships, not projects. Remember the old quote: "People don't care about how much you know until they know how much you care."

Relationships are marathons, not fast-food drive-thrus. Unfortunately, many people don't and won't change. But you're not responsible "for" them, you're responsible "to" them.

Questions I'm asking myself:
- Do I focus more on what I want to say to people or do I focus on genuinely caring for people?
- Am I living a life that is attractional? Do people see something positive and different in my life?
- Do I really spend time praying for those in my circles?
- Do I invite people to engage in a greater purpose—maybe as simple as a fundraising dinner or a small work project?
- Am I even reaching out to meet new people? When was the last time I had a new person or couple over for dinner?
- Would people say I'm encouraging and a "tank filler," or am I self-absorbed or a "tank drainer"?

God, help me to genuinely love people as You have loved us.

are fun-filled trips that any group of secular young professionals could take, but for the young Adventists who run Simply Missions, these weekends provide an invaluable opportunity for bonding with their non-believing peers and for sharing on a deeper level.

After two years of ministry, Reylourd and his group of leaders found that one of the key areas that engages young professionals is diet and health. Simply Missions explored the idea of adding a "better lifestyle movement" to its line-up of ministries. The plan it developed included opening a healthy food kiosk—a place where Adventist young people could show people healthy diet principles in practice, rather than just talking about them. With the support of the Pasay Adventist church and the Central Luzon Conference, Simply Foods, a vegan and vegetarian restaurant in a high-traffic, exclusive harbor-front shopping complex, does a brisk trade offering convenient, affordable fresh food.

It's easy to get lost in the flow chart of the Simply Missions ministries (which is found at www.simplymissionsph.org), but there has been a clear logic to its growth. Every aspect of Simply Missions circles around the central goal of connecting with a very specific demographic slice of Metro Manila. Manila's young professionals care about their work-life balance, health, diet and fitness, and their social life. So these are the areas in which Simply Missions has naturally developed. Aesthetics are also important in reaching out to this group. In everything it does, Simply Missions is conscious of image and design—from its printed material to the stylish façade of the Simply Foods kiosk, to the cafés where the CAFÉ Life groups meet, to the venues of the EPIC weekends.

The "front end" of Simply Missions—the part first seen by the young people it's trying to reach—has a distinctively casual feel. Those invited to attend a Simply Missions event or meet-up won't suddenly find themselves in uncomfortable territory, such as a traditional church setting. The CAFÉ Life gatherings operate in a way that feels organic and natural—almost like a spontaneous get-together of good friends. It's a vibe reinforced by Simply Missions' heavy reliance on social media for organizing and building a sense of community.

Yet when talking with Reylourd, it quickly becomes clear that the "back end" of Simply Missions is highly conceptualized in terms of its structure, mission, and theological rationale. Even names have significance: the word *café* in CAFÉ Life stands for "community, authenticity, friendship, experience," all essential planks in the Simply Missions approach to sharing Jesus in the city.

LIVING THE GOSPEL

Reylourd didn't set out to create a new ministry; it was born out of his personal spiritual journey and his growing conviction that God could use the youth of the Adventist Church in a unique way to engage with their postmodern and secular peers.

Before the birth of Simply Missions, Reylourd considered himself a typical pastor. He regularly conducted evangelistic series, and he reached his yearly baptismal goal. He was a firm believer in small groups and had implemented a strong small-group ministry in his churches.

Yet, Reylourd had a niggling awareness that in one essential aspect he was lacking. As a pastor whose job it is to share the gospel, Reylourd knew he wasn't very good at talking and mixing with non-believers. In fact, he readily admits that he was downright bad at it.

Reylourd had attended Adventist schools all his life. He was comfortable within the Adventist culture. He knew the "language," he understood the mindset, he resonated

A FRESH SERVE OF MINISTRY

The self-proclaimed mission of Simply Foods, the attractive outdoor kiosk café in Metro Manila's Harbor Square, is "Refashioning people's attitude toward healthy eating." But it's about much more than just the food. If you visit Simply Foods early on a Sunday morning, for instance, you could perhaps join an exercise class in progress, enjoy a vegetarian food tasting, attend a health workshop, watch a cooking demonstration, or receive a free heart check-up. Or you could just eat breakfast.

The casual café meshes with the Simply Mission ethos of focusing on what interests young urban professionals and is part of its Better Lifestyle Movement. Pastor Reylourd Reyes, who visits the kiosk every Tuesday to encourage the staff and every Sunday to interact with customers, says it provides a natural connection point with the very people he and his team hope to reach. To get a better sense of the scope of this vibrant ministry, go to www.facebook.com/SimplyFoodsPH.

with other Adventists' experiences, he shared their goals. But in groups of secular young people, he was frequently at a loss for words.

In 2010, while serving as the district pastor in Pampanga, his now-fiancée Carmi asked him a question. On its face, it was a simple question—one that should have been well within the ability of a young pastor to answer. Yet, it initially stumped Reylourd and ultimately prompted a turning point in his ministry.

Carmi was studying to become a doctor, and she asked Reylourd, "How can I tell my fellow medical students about Jesus?"

She'd already tried to share her faith with one of her classmates but had wound up only annoying her. "It won't work this way," said Carmi, "just sharing our Adventist beliefs and proving we're right from the Bible. We can't win them that way."

Carmi's words stuck with Reylourd. He started to wonder if Carmi was right. What if there was an entire segment of society—young, smart, educated Filipinos—who would never be attracted to Adventism via traditional outreach methods. And if this group really was slipping through the cracks of Adventist witness, then what could be done about it? Were these young people simply lost to God and His truth?

The following year, 2011, Reylourd left his more rural district to take up a new position as associate pastor at Pasay Adventist church, located inside Manila's endless urban sprawl. He was glad the move brought him closer to where Carmi was studying at the University of the East medical school. Often he'd find himself meeting up with Carmi and her medical-student friends at a café or restaurant and spending the evening just talking, getting to know these young men and women—not as secular, "un-churched people" or "non-Adventists," but simply as individuals.

One night, one of the regulars at their get-togethers asked Reylourd, "What do I do now? My parents just got separated." Reylourd suddenly realized that these medical students sitting around the table with him were simply people who had needs—needs that could be met by the Master Healer. "I realized that I needed to just hang out with them, like Jesus did, and meet their needs," says Reylourd.

And so in a sense, "hanging out with people" became the founding principle of the idea that became Simply Missions.

BELONG, *THEN* BELIEVE

When asked to describe the main difference between Simply Missions and some other forms of evangelism, Reylourd doesn't hesitate. "The difference is, this is not just a program," he says. "Being involved in mission isn't just a one-time event; mission is an approach to life that's shaped by our relationship with Jesus. It's about building relationships with others."

At Simply Missions, says Reylourd, "we invite people to belong first, even before they believe." Nurturing a sense of belonging and building community taps into a need that's deeply felt by many young urban professionals in Manila, he says.

Interestingly, the pull of community is probably just as important for the Adventist young people who are involved in various aspects of Simply Missions. They're experiencing—many for the first time—the joy of being involved in outreach to their peers. Perhaps they've felt underutilized in the past, or too inexperienced to take part in their church's evangelistic programs. Perhaps they've thought they didn't have the right skill set for witnessing. As part of the Simply Missions team, these Adventist young people are finding out that God can and will use whatever they offer Him. And in the process, their sense of connection to their faith and their church is growing stronger.

Some 90 Adventist young people are regularly engaged with Simply Missions, helping facilitate more than a dozen CAFÉ Life groups, running the ever-popular EPIC Weekends, and opening up God's Word to people in Grow Groups and Growth Groups.

"WHY I KEEP COMING BACK"

Perhaps the greatest reward for Reylourd and his Simply Missions team is the knowledge they're building a genuine, Christ-infused community among a group of people who otherwise would have no interest in hearing about Jesus, let alone the Adventist Church.

Donj, 24, Raphael, 26, and Daven, 25, are three urbanites who could never have imagined themselves forming such a close bond with a group of Christians. These three young professionals are part of a group that meets every Wednesday evening in Makati just to chat and check in on each other. "It's casual, light!" says Donj. "For me, it's a clean way to spend my Wednesdays."

Before encountering Simply Missions, Donj says he was "trapped in the common majority" of working professionals his age. "On payday you go out to drink—that's a typical hangout. But when I started attending Project Grow, [I learned] particularly from the people I'm with, that it's possible to have clean fun, and to get closer to God and the people around you."

"They make us feel that we belong," says Daven, "that what we do matters." Daven commutes two hours each Wednesday to the Project Grow meeting. He says that when other friends hear about the level of his commitment to the weekly meeting, they wonder why he does it. "I always tell them, 'It's because I see the people here. They really are sincere in what they do. They really care for you.' "

Daven, who now regularly prays and reads the Bible, says, "I can see that it benefits me."

What stands out for Raphael is the attitude of the people he meets. "The community is refreshing," he says. "They are very genuine in what they do. They're just who they are. They've never pushed me to change anything about my lifestyle."

"There's a saying, 'Put charcoal with charcoal and you'll also be on fire,' " adds Raphael. "That's kind of like why I keep coming back."

Donj sums it up: "The people of this community are inspiring because they inspire by example. I see their lifestyle, I see how they work, and how they treat other people. They never said, 'You should be exactly like this.' They never did that. I just saw their example and I was inspired. I wanted to be like them."

SOCIAL NETWORKING FOR GOD'S KINGDOM
Lessons from the front lines of urban mission

- **Offer acceptance.** Before offering people anything, offer them your acceptance. Provide them a social and emotional home base—a community. And then introduce them to Jesus and His plans for them.
- **Activate and engage Adventist young people**—not just for the sake of the mission work but also their own spiritual development.
- **Accept the responsibility of witnessing.** The responsibility of being a witness for Jesus belongs to everyone, not just to pastors. Consider Ellen White's words, "The greatest help that can be given our people is to teach them to work for God, and to depend on Him, not on the ministers."[1]
- **Show people the gospel.** Then they'll be more open to you telling them the gospel. Your life is your first witness.
- **Be prepared to adapt.** Traditional evangelism still reaches many people, but look for those it bypasses, and be prepared to adapt your approach—significantly, if necessary. Reworking outreach methods isn't compromising truth, just repackaging the way it's communicated.
- **Get to know them.** People aren't statistics or targets, they're people. Get to know them well. Friendship makes many things possible.

---

1 *Testimonies for the Church*, 7:19.

SHOWING SYMPATHY

"THE SAVIOR MINGLED WITH MEN
AS ONE WHO DESIRED
THEIR GOOD. HE SHOWED
HIS *SYMPATHY* FOR THEM."

ELLEN G. WHITE

"JESUS MINISTERED TO PEOPLE ACCORDING TO THEIR NEEDS. He showed heartfelt sympathy towards individuals even when they did not quite grasp what God's kingdom is about. Do we lovingly care for people irrespective of their ultimately becoming disciples? Do we allow God to reach to us through their lives and minister to us as we also minister to them? Are we open to give through receiving? I believe what people need most is genuine love that is expressed through personal care, investment of time, energy, heartfelt empathy, and mutual friendship."

Simret Mahary *is pastor and director of PRESENCE kulturlounge, an urban Center of Influence in Frankfurt/Main, Germany.*

"In one of the churches I planted, we asked God to send us the people that nobody wants. Rather than merely sharing our bread with the less fortunate, we decided to share our lives. We befriended Pam, who was living in chronic homelessness and came out of the woods every Sabbath to worship and eat with us. She spoke about her dream to become an artist and her frustrations in not realizing it. We helped her start a cash business painting t-shirts for $10 each, from which she tithed cash on Sabbath.

"That business enabled her to purchase a bicycle and, more importantly, pursue her dreams. She eventually accepted Jesus, in part because we entered into her world. The sympathy of Jesus does that."

Anthony WagenerSmith *is a church planter, church planting coordinator, and pastor of LifeSpring Adventist Church in Tampa, United States.*

CHAPTER 3

ABANDON ASSUMPTIONS HERE

The question "How can we serve you?"
yields surprising answers for one city ministry.

BETTINA KRAUSE

*E*LLEN WHITE WROTE, *"To reach people, wherever they are, and whatever their position or condition, and to help them in every way possible—this is true ministry."*[1] What would happen if Seventh-day Adventists really took her words to heart and put them into practice? One group of dedicated urban missionaries is finding out.

ALLENTOWN, PENNSYLVANIA, UNITED STATES

When it came, the reality check was brutal. For some 14 months, the Simplicity Outreach Center team in Allentown, Pennsylvania, had been visiting and studying with Natasha,[2] a young mother scarred by a difficult past and failed relationships. Since Simplicity had been establishing a Center of Influence in this economically struggling area of Allentown, the main focus of its ministry had been services to the children and young people of the neighborhood—after-school programs, a community garden, worship services on Sabbath. Natasha was one of the few adults who had expressed interest in Bible studies. She'd formed a close bond with the members of the missionary team; she volunteered with various Simplicity programs, and she attended church on Sabbath.

And then Natasha expressed interest in baptism. For Wes Via, who was then director of the Simplicity Outreach Center, it was a moment to savor—this was some much-needed reassurance that God's Spirit was indeed working through the efforts of his team to reach this neighborhood for Christ.

---

1 *The Ministry of Healing,* 156.
2 This name has been changed.

There was just one problem. Natasha had a live-in boyfriend. She'd said before that she knew it wasn't a good situation for her and she wanted to leave the relationship. But for now it seemed that everything was in a holding pattern.

One evening, Wes and his wife visited Natasha and sat listening as her words flowed out. She unloaded a weight of past hurts and traumas: a controlling relationship, emotional abuse, and more. Carefully, gently, Wes showed Natasha that her current live-in relationship wasn't in line with biblical principles. He pledged his and the team's support as she did what she needed to do in order to deal with the situation. "We'll be with you every step of the way," Wes promised.

Natasha's response was immediate—and it was negative. She stopped coming to church, and she broke off contact with Wes, although other members of the Simplicity team continued their efforts to stay in touch. Later—much later—after Wes had suffered and prayed and had slowly come to a deeper understanding of God's expectations for him and the Simplicity project, Natasha finally confided what she had experienced that night.

She'd known the status of her relationship stood in the way of her baptism. But that evening, she'd opened herself and bared her emotions in a way that left her feeling deeply vulnerable. For her, Wes's response had fallen short of the mark. "Later, she told us what she'd needed was for us to pray with her," says Wes. "To let her know that we'd really heard what she'd confided, that we understood the larger picture of what was going on in her life, and what had happened in her past."

"She'd entrusted all this to us," adds Wes, "and yet we focused only on the narrower issue." At the time, Wes thought he was simply affirming her feeling that it was time to change her relationship—bolstering her resolve with biblical support. "She interpreted all this, though, as us being 'pushy.' She felt we'd missed most of what she'd said, and we were focused on getting her to do what we wanted her to do."

Although his relationship with Natasha was ultimately restored, the experience brought home to Wes, clearly and painfully, that reaching people for Christ in the difficult mission field of the city often requires an added measure of patience, sensitivity, and compassion. And most of all, it demands an unwavering, laser-like focus on individuals and their needs—physical, emotional, and spiritual.

"My work with Simplicity has been revolutionary for me, personally," says Wes, who has since moved on to another ministry. "I came from a traditional evangelism mindset of trying to figure out how to get people through the doors of the church. And so I had to fight the urge to apply a one-size-fits-all approach.

"My focus has shifted and, for me, the most important thing now is to teach people how to have a relationship with God and how to read their Bible meaningfully," says Wes. "God can use that and build on that. Even if they don't make a decision for Christ right then, maybe God will call them to pick up the Bible sometime in the future. And when they do, they'll know how to engage with God through His Word."

A FIVE-BLOCK MISSION FIELD

Dr. Jeff McAuliffe, a Seventh-day Adventist layperson, is the driving force behind Simplicity—a Center of Influence model of ministry that is transforming the Pennsylvania Conference's approach to urban outreach. Jeff's early research was mainly within the writings of Ellen White, where he uncovered a massive amount of counsel that the church should focus on the cities as a primary mission target. Later, he developed a complementary biblical approach for city outreach based on the apostle Paul's experience in Ephesus, recorded in Acts 19 and 20.

Over a period of two or three years, Jeff continued to share the results of his research with the Pennsylvania Conference Executive Committee. Soon, Conference leaders had also caught the vision for urban outreach and committed themselves to getting Simplicity off the ground. They chose to begin their efforts in Allentown.

Allentown is a city surrounded and dwarfed by even larger cities. Fifty miles southeast of Allentown is Philadelphia, the fifth largest city in the United States; 90 miles to the east lies New York City, the nation's largest city; and, some 90 miles to the west is the state capital, Harrisburg. Allentown itself is a part of the so-called Rust Belt of America—those cities that enjoyed a manufacturing boom in the 1800s and 1900s, but which have been dealt with less kindly by the economic realities of recent decades.

Perhaps nowhere in Allentown is this economic decline more apparent than in Ward 8, the city district where Simplicity Outreach Center established its ministry in 2012. The area has a large number of recent immigrants, many with a Hispanic heritage, and many who don't speak English. Residents tend to work two or three low-paying jobs just to stay financially afloat and to keep their children housed and fed.

The original Simplicity team, Jeff, Wes, and three young Bible workers, mapped out a zone measuring about a five-block radius from their premises, and this became their new mission territory. Jeff had learned from other non-profits in Allentown that the impact of a service or agency usually extended only as far as people could easily walk, or were willing to allow their children to walk alone.

The key to Jeff's approach lies in the name of the project: Simplicity. The uncomplicated goal of the project is simply to make meaningful connections with people in a specific neighborhood—through friendship and through meeting real needs—and thus to reveal Christ and His love. Or, as Wes has put it, "At Simplicity we believe the essence of Christ's method of ministry is to display the gospel before you tell the gospel."

But "simple" does not necessarily equate with "easy." If the ministry team wanted to meet the real needs of the community, they first needed to find out what those needs were. And that involved the grind of knocking on doors and talking to people, house after house, day after day, developing an intimate understanding of what drives this particular section of Allentown.

The Simplicity missionaries walked along the streets of redbrick row houses, some in good repair, others bearing signs of neglect. When they knocked on a door, they

BEING CHRIST'S HANDS AND FEET IN ALLENTOWN

Lessons from the front lines of urban mission

- **Find meaningful points of contact in community.** Just say "Hi" to people and get to know them. Visit them. Be present, active, and engaged in community matters.
- **Get to know your mission field—intimately.** Research its demographics, talk to other nonprofit or governmental agencies working in the area, and research its history and culture. Understand its undercurrents and daily rhythms.
- **Allow your ministry to grow organically.** Offer what people want and value, rather than what you think they should want and value.
- **Get rid of the idea that there's a definite "right" and "wrong" way to do things.** And let go of the idea that you need to rely on a pastor or paid mission worker to get things done. God has given people passion, gifts, and vision for Christ's mission. So find ways to funnel that passion into direct ministry.
- **Focus on Christ's method of ministry.** It takes time, it doesn't produce overnight results, but the Holy Spirit blesses and brings "fruit" in His own time.

held in their hand a checklist of services that Simplicity could potentially provide—child care, after-school programs, health or educational programs, help with the home or garden. Their goal was to get hard data that would allow Simplicity to offer targeted services, rather than wasting time and resources on unneeded and unwanted programs.

In Jeff's model, this period of research is fundamental. Wes draws parallels between urban ministry and cross-cultural mission work. Missionaries traveling to other countries dig deep into the culture of their new territory; they're intent on understanding the nuances of the language, philosophy, and mindset of those they're trying to reach for Christ. The cross-cultural missionary takes a long-term view and isn't focused on quick results. Their goal is to establish a presence within the foreign territory that will continue to grow organically, long after the missionary has returned home.

The door-to-door needs assessment Simplicity undertook was prompted by this same desire to engage the community in a deep and genuine way. The missionaries asked residents, "How safe is your neighborhood?" "What's the greatest need in the community?" "Is there anything we can do for you, personally?"

What the Simplicity missionaries found after they'd compiled the results of their hard-won data determined the shape of their future ministry in Allentown. They discovered that many hardworking, cash-poor residents of this community were so busy providing the basics of life for their children that they couldn't give them an equally important commodity—their time. Thus, children and young people were often left to their own devices while adults worked multiple jobs. One of the key needs in the community was for after-school and weekend programs for kids.

DONOVAN AND MICHELLE
BY WES VIA

With a full belly and a smile on his face, nine-year-old Donovan climbed in the front seat of Bekah's car. Bekah, one of our missionaries at the Simplicity Outreach Center in Allentown, Pennsylvania, was giving Donovan and some of his friends a ride home from a cooking class we had hosted.

Donovan didn't pay much attention to the lively chatter in the back seat until someone cursed. Then he immediately turned around and said in a kind yet serious tone, "You shouldn't talk like that, we're in the presence of God!" Pretty incredible words for a boy who had only recently learned about Jesus.

We first met Donovan when he came to our children's brunch. It was there that he heard his first Bible story. Two months later, he joined our children's Bible study, where he learned that God loves him and wants to give him eternal life. Donovan excitedly accepted the gospel invitation, and the change in his life has been dramatic.

The day Andrew, a Simplicity missionary, and Reyes, a local church member, knocked on Michelle's door, she had to force herself off the couch. Six days earlier she had been thrown in jail while her four children were forcibly removed from her home due to a false allegation. To say she was depressed would be an understatement.

Andrew and Reyes told Michelle they were taking a survey to discover how Simplicity could serve the needs of the community. Michelle filled out the survey and then began to open up about what was happening in her life. Reyes, who is a mother herself, asked whether she could pray for Michelle.

Michelle told us later that she had only accepted Reyes's offer for prayer because she didn't want to be rude. "I wasn't a Christian at the time, and I didn't believe in prayer," she says. "But as Reyes prayed, I felt peace and a strong impression that I would get my children back." The next day that is exactly what happened. Michelle has been eagerly studying the Bible and volunteering at Simplicity ever since.

Donovan lived in the apartment below Michelle's for a while, so Michelle knew him before he started coming to Simplicity. "I can't believe he's the same kid," says Michelle. "I never let my kids play with him before, but he's totally different now!"[1]

You can find out more about the Simplicity Outreach Center at www.simplicityyoutreach.org.

---

1 Adapted from *Mission 360* magazine and used with permission.

By default, Adventist outreach often leans toward health-related seminars or programs. Yet it soon became clear that the time-challenged residents of Ward 8 would be unlikely to leave their homes of an evening or weekend to attend programs such as these.

The door-to-door surveys did quickly unearth one unexpected community need, though—English-language training for recent immigrants.

However, even with this, the Simplicity team learned a hard lesson in staying tuned to the rhythms of the neighborhood. Once they'd identified English as a second language (ESL) classes as a primary need, they set about arranging a teacher and advertising classes. To their surprise, only 12 people signed up, only six people actually attended on the first night, and eventually just four graduated.

What had gone wrong? For their next attempt at offering ESL classes, Simplicity acquired the services of an experienced local ESL teacher who managed to clear up the mystery. Simplicity had offered their classes too early in the evening, making it difficult for working parents to get home, do chores, and get to class on time. With the second round of classes, Simplicity moved the starting time to half an hour later, and the ESL classes took off.

A "BESPOKE MINISTRY"

In creating an urban Center of Influence such as Simplicity, it's natural to want to find and follow a blueprint for ministry, says Wes. "Its tempting to think that if I just follow a particular model that's worked elsewhere—follow step A, B, C and D—then I'll have success. We want to extrapolate directly from one context to another.

"But that is not the nature of wholistic outreach—Christ's ministry—which must always be responsive to the culture in which it's located," he adds. "Even within one city, such as New York, the needs of people in the Bronx won't be the same as those in Manhattan or Brooklyn." Thus, understanding the micro-cultures within cities is crucial to tailoring services that connect with the community and to building trust.

One consequence of this reality is that urban mission will inevitably take longer to accomplish. Programs can't be imported in a "pre-fabricated" form. They have to be built from the ground up.

The first programs that Simplicity built in Allentown were focused on the number-one need they identified in the community—activities for children and young people. They started with the 6–11 year-old age group, but after a time noticed that 13- and 14-year-olds were coming in too. So Simplicity added activities for that age group, and so the roster of programs began to grow naturally. The small number of kids who first started dropping in to the center became Simplicity's best recruiters, inviting their friends and siblings. Each week, the Simplicity Outreach Center continues to host various after-school activities: including tutoring, cooking classes a couple of times a week, and a youth group that meets regularly. On Tuesdays the missionaries and the kids work together in a nearby community garden, and on Sabbaths there's a kids' brunch following the morning program.

Members of the Simplicity team also began making twice-monthly visits to the home of each of child who attended programs at the center. This way, they were able to start making connections among the adult members of the community, getting to know parents and caregivers, talking to them about their kids, and slowly building trust.

Before adding new programming, the leaders of Simplicity wait until those they serve bring a significant need to their attention. "Our benchmark is usually eight to ten people asking for something repeatedly over the course of six weeks or so before we start anything new," says Wes. "We want natural growth."

This natural growth approach has led to after-school tutoring, summer day camps, kids' cooking classes, wellness groups, yard care for busy residents, and many more finely targeted programs.

WANTED: URBAN MISSIONARIES

Another important value for Simplicity is to build up a network of community volunteers—not just among believers, but everyone who wants to do something positive for the community. "What we're doing here doesn't require a heavy theological foundation," says Wes. "It requires a very practical, human foundation of recognizing what people need."

And this approach also brings non-believers within the ambit of Simplicity and offers an opportunity to share Christ with fellow volunteers. Several community volunteers have already asked the Simplicity team for Bible studies. "For some people, allowing them to be the hands of Christ is the way to their hearts," says Jeff.

He says that one of their more interesting groups of community volunteers is a local biker gang. "They come out on a regular basis and help us with various ministries." The bikers' association with Simplicity began a couple of years ago during a holiday event, where the missionaries planned to give out clothes and food donations to the community.

"There weren't a lot of people showing up," recalls Jeff, "but one of our volunteers said, 'I know a group of guys and gals who are really into this kind of thing.'" Before long the low rumble of motorcycles announced the arrival of the most "imposing" group of volunteers the Simplicity team had ever encountered. Before long, the bikers' presence had completely revived Simplicity's holiday event.

"Just recently, one of the biker couples asked us, out the blue, whether they could become members of our church," says Jeff. "They're in Bible studies and in church each Sabbath simply because they decided to volunteer with Simplicity."

Simplicity also aims to refute the idea that Adventist church members should sit back and let "experts" do ministry and mission. "The apostles weren't paid clergymen," Wes points out. "They were basically knowledgeable laymen who made ministry their first priority. They supported themselves so they could do ministry wherever they were at the time."

Grassroots support from six local Adventist churches is crucial to the ongoing success of Simplicity and, in turn, the project has become a place where church members can learn and practice hands-on ministry. Wes says that one of the great joys of his time as project director was "seeing church members 'get it,' and become supportive and engage with us; seeing the tears in their eyes during the debriefing process; hearing them say, 'This is so meaningful.' "

But some traditional forms of support haven't been quite as helpful. Wes recalls one program they ran where, for the first few nights, local Adventists showed up in force to "flesh out" the audience. After the third meeting, though, Adventist attendance dropped off sharply, leaving the three remaining non-Adventist attendees sitting in the near-empty room, feeling somewhat bemused.

TAKING THE LONG VIEW

"God takes care of the big picture," says Jeff. "Sometimes when I speak at different places, people ask me, 'How are you going to reach the city?' And I say, 'Well, that's not my job. Our job is to do what's right there in front of us.' "

Today, Simplicity missionaries are studying the Bible with 32 people in the neighborhood, and within the space of just a few weeks in early 2015, six people requested baptism. Recently, four more local residents requested Bible studies following an Easter cantata put on by children who regularly participate with Simplicity.

The Pennsylvania Conference has recently approved the addition of a church school to the outreach center, which will serve non-Adventist children from Allentown's Ward 8. Jeff says their goal will be to make tuition "very affordable" and to provide sponsorships for students whose family can't afford even these nominal fees. Already, the Conference has hired a teacher for the school. With this effort, Simplicity is following Ellen White's counsel to establish church schools in the cities: "Much more can be done to save and educate the children of those who at present cannot get away from the cities," she wrote. "This is a matter worthy of our best efforts."[3]

As he looks even further into the future, Jeff says they'd like to establish a free health clinic for Ward 8 residents, which would be a much-needed service for the community. The Conference's long-term plan also includes opening more Simplicity Outreach Centers in other wards of Allentown and other cities of Pennsylvania.

For now, Jeff believes the Simplicity Outreach Center is modeling the type of urban mission, solidly grounded on biblical principles and Ellen White's counsel, that can break through some of the barriers that obstruct traditional evangelism in urban settings. People too busy to attend meetings? Not interested in spiritual things? Too stressed just trying to make ends meet? By simply asking, "How can we serve you?" Simplicity is turning these "negatives" into connection points with their community.

---

3 *Child Guidance*, 306.

It's hard work, it's a long-term proposition, and the results, in terms of baptisms, may not be as dramatic as seen in some other places. But day after day, one home visit and after-school program at a time, Simplicity is bringing Christ's healing, loving presence to the streets of this city. And for Jeff and his team of missionaries, this is more than enough.

CHAPTER 4

IF CHRIST WALKED THE STREETS OF NAIROBI

Seeing people and their needs through
Christ's eyes is the very first step.

CATHERINE NYAMEINO

*I*T CAN FEEL OVERWHELMING. *Around you there's so much human suffering, so many people walking past you on the city streets, each one of whom desperately needs to know their Creator and Savior. You could let yourself become paralyzed by the vastness of the challenge. Or you could do what one group of Kenyan Seventh-day Adventists chose to do: use the resources they had in their hands to start transforming lives—one at a time.*

As the sun goes down in the backstreets of Kenya's capital, Nairobi, a decades-old ritual begins. Among the crowds of people making their way home after work each day are those who have a different destination in mind. In dusty, narrow alleyways, doors open and men enter houses seeking temporary escape from the grinding reality of their everyday lives. They pay their money and sit down, sometimes alone, sometimes around a communal pot, sipping through "straws" of hollowed-out electrical cords. They are drinking homemade alcohol—illicit brews such as *changaa* or *busaa*—that are fermented in home stills from grains such as sorghum, millet, and wheat. These small, unlicensed "pubs" that dot the city and its outlying suburbs dispense potent brews that are sometimes adulterated with deadly quantities of gasoline, battery acid, or other toxic ingredients in an attempt to give the drink an extra "kick."

The word *changaa*, literally interpreted, means "kill me quick," and it sometimes lives up to its name. Newspapers frequently report incidences of violent illness, blindness, and death caused by drinking these noxious brews, and yet the popularity of Nairobi's drinking dens remains undiminished. For thousands upon thousands in this city, they offer an affordable, if dangerous, alternative to commercially produced alcohol, which poverty has placed beyond the reach of many Kenyans.

The impact of these illicit brews is devastating both to individuals and to the community. Beyond the headlines of death and injury from bad batches, there are thousands of untold stories of pain: jobs lost, families destroyed, health and self-respect ruined, communities disintegrating.

A NEW STRATEGY

The Seventh-day Adventist Church's East Kenya Union Conference, based in Nairobi, considered how it could implement the world church's Mission to the Cities initiative. How could Adventists in this urban sprawl introduce Christ's method of reaching people? How could they show Christ's compassion in practical ways? How could they help guide people toward a path of spiritual and physical wholeness? Union leaders first developed a strategic plan that identified some of the most challenging groups found in the city, including sex workers, street families, drug addicts, slum dwellers, those with lifestyle diseases, those with broken relationships, and communities with high rates of crime. Church leaders quickly recognized also that an almost-constant feature of every community in the city was the pervasive and destructive use of illicit brews.

As they contemplated the vast challenge before them, union leaders cast a vision for starting urban centers of influence, which would introduce Christ's method of reaching people on the streets of Nairobi. It wasn't long before churches and lay leaders around the city began to take up the challenge.

GABRIEL'S STORY

On the outskirts of Nairobi, some 10 miles from the city center, lies a suburb known as Wangige. The central Wangige market is renowned for its colorful displays of fresh produce and its bustling atmosphere, which attracts fruit and vegetable sellers from surrounding areas. And yet, ironically, a village known for its fresh fruit and vegetables is also a place where a majority of the population engages in drinking illicit brews, smoking, and drug abuse.

Gabriel Maina is an elder of King'eero Seventh-day Adventist Church in Wangige, and he has a passion to change people's lives. Since 1993, he has been a stalwart in a church-run ministry to those with HIV and AIDS, and he formed a support group for HIV-positive men and women that continues today, more than 20 years later.

When Gabriel heard about the Mission to the Cities initiative, he immediately thought of those in his town whose lives were controlled by their addiction to illicit brews. For him, the problem had a personal dimension. His son had once come home drunk, confronting Gabriel with the terrible power of these illegal brews and with the possibility that he could lose his own child to drinking.

Gabriel approached Pastor Samuel Lumwe, director of the Office of Adventist Mission in East Kenya and the Mission to the Nairobi City coordinator, and requested financial support for a new ministry to combat the power of illicit brews in Wangige.

BRINGING THE CHURCH
TO THE CITY MARKETPLACE

Lessons from the front lines of urban mission

- **Don't rush.** Leading people to God cannot be a hurried process. It is important to mingle, make friends, meet physical needs, and then prayerfully introduce them to Him.
- **Where possible, empower people.** Through the HIV/Aids project, rejected and helpless women and men have become Christians with a strong support group and sustainable income-generating projects. When people become self-reliant financially, they become good examples to others.
- **Start small—and prayerfully.** Our responsibility is to take the first steps of faith, to sow the seeds. It is God's responsibility to grow our ministries in His own time, at His own pace.
- **Use all your available resources.** Ask, "What do I have in my hands?" Even when you've identified a community need, you may feel you don't have enough resources to do something meaningful. But remember, this is God's business, and if you simply use what you have in your hands, He will bless it.
- **Don't forget the ultimate goal.** Don't forget that the task is incomplete until people have not only quit bad habits but have also given their lives to the Saviour.

Then, with support from Pastor Lumwe and the Union office, Gabriel embarked on his new venture.

He began small, with a personal, low-key approach. He gathered a group of volunteers from King'eero church who had worked together for years in the church's HIV ministry, and they began visiting illegal drinking dens and other places where illicit brews are served.

One well-known place in Wangige where illegal alcohol is often sold is called Base, where groups of unemployed men gather each day and wait for prospective employers. Gabriel and his team mingled with the men at Base, chatting with them and striking up conversations. And then they issued a simple invitation. Anyone who wanted to quit drinking, smoking, and drug abuse was welcome to come to a meeting at the local marketplace the following Wednesday. In a short time, more than a hundred people had accepted the invitation and, on the day of the meeting, the tent Gabriel had hired for the event was filled to overflowing. For regulars in the marketplace, it was astounding to see so many drinkers of illicit brews gathered together publicly in one place.

Leaders kept the meeting format simple, beginning with singing familiar Christian choruses, prayers, and then a number of health talks. Among the speakers were local village elders and church leaders, but perhaps the most powerful speeches of the day were given by a number of the drinkers themselves. They talked about the many different challenges they faced, the circumstances that had brought them to this place, and their deep desire to escape the power of alcohol addiction. One man's testimony was particularly moving. He said that, until that day, "We have never known that someone loves us."

After the meeting, church volunteers provided lunch, and it soon became clear that the simple act of sharing food was a potent way of breaking down social barriers.

"As we served food together with the drunkards, I started to notice a lot of easiness amongst them," said Gabriel. "They mingled with us much more easily than when we addressed them from the podium."

Before the gathering broke up, Gabriel and his team distributed *Discover* Bible lessons and invited everyone back for another meeting the following week.

The following Wednesday, Gabriel and his team set up the tent in the marketplace and waited to see if any would return. They were delighted when 80 of the original attendees came back.

At the first meeting, leaders had noticed that many of the men were poorly dressed, so at this second meeting, they distributed clothes and shoes donated by church members. By the fourth meeting, it was clear that this rehabilitation ministry would be a long-term project, and so to save the expense of hiring a tent each week, the participants agreed to move the gatherings to the King'eero Adventist church compound. Today, this is where the ministry is based and where church members continue to welcome the illicit-brew drinkers of Wangige.

KEVIN'S STORY

The church members of King'eero Adventist church are discovering that the road to rehabilitation for those addicted to alcohol and drugs is long and difficult. Yet a core group of committed individuals continue to attend meetings at the church each week, and a number of them have been able to quit their old habits completely.

Thirty-year-old Kevin Edwin Boro was one of the original attendees of the rehabilitation meetings in Wangige marketplace. Before his life took a downward spiral, his future had once held great promise. After high school, Kevin earned a higher national diploma in information technology, and he hoped to build a career in this field. Yet after a long, fruitless search for a full-time job, he gave up and started looking for casual jobs just to earn enough money to get by. Kevin started to join other job seekers each day at Base, and before long he had made friends with people who regularly drank illicit brews.

"I found myself in wrong company, and before long I started to drink to drown my problems," he says. "After a while I started smoking and then went into hard drugs." Inevitably, a terrible cycle developed. The more problems Kevin faced, the more he drank to escape them, which, in turn, made him less able to deal with challenges.

"You know, drinking makes one feel like all is well, but in reality, things get worse," he says.

When the volunteers from King'eero Adventist church came to Base in 2014 talking about a new program for drinkers of illicit brew, Kevin immediately recognized a lifeline. "I needed something better, and the invitation was like a Godsend," he says. "I seized the opportunity and went for that first meeting, and have not stopped attending since then. I have now quit all those habits, and I feel much better."

When asked what particularly attracted him to the group, Kevin says, "It was the love that they showed us. And every time I attend the meetings, I experience a lot of peace within me. Sometimes I don't feel like leaving. They pray for us and speak to us so well."

"I am still young, and I now realize I was wasting my life away," he adds. "I realize that all along I was in a state of denial, and I now need to face the reality of the dangers of my former habits." With the help and encouragement of his mentors, Kevin is now looking forward to starting a new life. He has attended the local Adventist church a few times since the first meeting, and he says he has found it "interesting."

JOHN'S STORY

John Mbugua is another person who thanks God he accepted Gabriel's invitation to attend the King'eero Adventist church rehabilitation meeting in the marketplace. John started drinking when he was 23 years old and now, at 28, he's only just beginning to realize the full extent of what he has lost over the past five years. As John's dependence on alcohol and drugs grew, his earnings as a trained carpenter began to disappear, and his wife and child often went hungry as John spent his evenings in illegal drinking dens. Eventually, John's wife moved out, and his carpentry customers deserted him. They could no longer trust John to complete their work properly or on time. John found himself without money, in bad company, and in increasingly desperate circumstances. He began to feel that, without drugs, he was nobody. Drugs and alcohol became his identity.

The first meeting of the rehabilitation group was a revelation to John. As he sat in the crowd of people and listened to the various speakers, he realized that there was a vast difference between his life and the lives of those who didn't drink or take drugs. In the weeks that followed, John has worked hard to change his habits, but it hasn't been easy. He admits that he still drinks, "but not as heavily as I used to before I joined the group."

"I am now working towards stopping completely," says John, "because I have realized that you can still live without drinking, smoking, and taking drugs."

DAVID'S STORY

Forty-five-year-old David Karanja Kibugi has also decided to quit drinking as a result of joining the King'eero church rehabilitation program. He started drinking in 2004, when he got his first job at a local butchery.

"I used to work late and, most evenings, our clients were those who drank at a neighboring bar," he says. "When I delivered meat to one particular customer, the person would invite me to drink one bottle. Before long I was hooked on drinking, and because I could not afford the beer, I started taking some drink that was packed in small sachets."

David's wife and three children have suffered greatly as a result of his drinking. "I picked quarrels very easily, and of course I could not provide for my family," says David. "When I came home, I often drank and was told there was no food. I could quarrel, but I knew I would eat at the butchery the following morning. My wife and children often went hungry."

David lost his job at the butchery but afterward began to learn the masonry trade.

"Although I am a good mason, I do not easily find jobs because prospective hirers would always find me drunk and could not give me any job," he says. David has now quit drinking, a decision he dates to the very first rehabilitation meeting he attended.

"Deep within, I had come to a point of wanting to quit but got stuck because I did not know how to do it on my own," he explains. "When I joined the group, however, and heard and saw how my fellow drunkards were equally frustrated and struggling with their habits, I decided that it was time to change my ways." David still struggles with smoking, although he has cut back and wants to stop entirely soon. The support he has found within the rehabilitation group allows David to envision a new future for himself, one in which his old destructive habits no longer have any power over him.

TRANSFORMATIONS

Kevin, John, and David each say that their drinking and drug habits spilled out into every facet of their lives and essentially separated them from the rest of society. They admit they've caused their families great distress and hardship, and they each look back with a sense of regret. Today, they continue to struggle financially, and they often go hungry. Yet, in the months since they've joined the King'eero church rehabilitation group, they have each seen significant changes in their lives, and, even more important, they now experience a new sense of belonging and love.

They attribute their new hope to the care of the local Adventist church, which, through Gabriel and his team, took interest in these "misfits" and reached out to them. Each week, they enjoy the meetings and the camaraderie, and say they'd often like to just stay in the church compound all the time, because this is where they've found love and acceptance.

As physical transformations take hold, Gabriel and the other leaders of the rehabilitation project are looking for ways to help the men take the next step to support themselves financially and to begin building a new life for themselves. Although Kevin, John, and David each have a professional skill, Gabriel says they need some start-up capital to launch themselves in business once again. In some cases, Gabriel says, providing "graduates" of the rehabilitation program with a reliable means of transportation, such as a motorcycle, could also be a way to help them restart their professional lives.

Alcohol and drugs continue to ravage lives, decimate families, and bring economic ruin on the streets of Nairobi, but members from the King'eero Seventh-day Adventist Church are lighting sparks of hope. And as they help meet the physical needs of those who are struggling, they are introducing them to the One who has power to truly transform every aspect of human life. The same One who is walking the streets of Nairobi beside them each step of the way.

CHAPTER 5

A HEART FOR COPENHAGEN:
BRINGING WARMTH TO A COLD WORLD

*A unique urban Center of Influence
becomes a point of connection in the community.*

GARY KRAUSE

*T*O SOME IT MAY SOUND INCONGRUOUS—*a second-hand store as a
Center of Influence within a city steeped in religious skepticism. How could that
work? Yet Seventh-day Adventists in Copenhagen are discovering how even a thrift
store can help build deep, genuine relationships within a community and take hope in Jesus
outside the four walls of the church.*

COPENHAGEN, DENMARK

The Assistens Cemetery dominates the neighborhood just outside the old Northern
Gate of Copenhagen, Denmark. Today this old burial place, a little northwest of the
city center, doubles as a city park where people come to relax, picnic, enjoy concerts,
and enjoy an oasis in the urban environment. Basking in the beauty of the park, they
can easily forget the more than 300,000 bodies buried beneath them, including two
of Denmark's most famous writers, Hans Christian Andersen and Søren Kierkegaard.
Also interred beneath the picnic blankets is Nobel Prize–winning physicist Niels Bohr,
who played a significant role in developing quantum mechanics and nuclear physics.

The longest street bordering this cemetery is Nørrebrogade, the cosmopolitan, pul-
sating main thoroughfare of Copenhagen's Nørrebro district. On the other side of
this street, one of the busiest in the city, a Seventh-day Adventist Center of Influence
operates under the engaging name of HappyHand. In many ways, HappyHand is a
counterpoint to the cemetery. Assistens, founded in 1760, is a memorial to the past;
HappyHand, founded in 2012, is all about sharing hope and a future. Assistens takes
up more than 60 acres of urban landscape; HappyHand is one small store. Assistens

DREAM BIG, WORK HARD, AND LET GOD DO THE REST

Lessons from the front lines of urban mission

- **Location**. "It's so important to find the right place, style and size—and then stick to it," says Anne-May. "We've learned that the location is very important. We have so many people walk by our shop every day—the location is ideal for a shop and project like ours. It took a lot of time to find the right place, but it's worth the wait. Do it right from the beginning."

- **Don't dream too small.** The HappyHand Center of Influence is 223 square meters (2,400 square feet). At first the leaders thought it was too big. "Now we know we could have used at least double the size!" says Anne-May.

- **Put Christ's method into practice.** The HappyHand Center of Influence provides the means for church members to mingle with people, show sympathy, minister to needs, win confidence, and bid people to follow Jesus. "We've created a natural platform for people to meet us and get a glimpse of God," says Anne-May. "This project is tearing down barriers between the average Dane and our church—and that's indeed a great joy."

- **Be prepared for hard work.** "HappyHand has been and still is a lot of hard work," says Berit. "It's a challenge to work with volunteers when you are a volunteer your-self. But thanks to God, the blessings are greater than the challenges."

- **Put your trust in God.** "Since the beginning of the project, we've been confident, knowing that this is God's project," says Berit. "We put it in the hands of God and pray that He will lead us to make the decisions that He wants us to."

- **Connect with people's interests.** "I've learned a lot about stewardship from the shoppers in HappyHand," says Thomas Müller. "They care about creation, they care about our natural resources, and they're conscious of not exploiting nature. They don't attribute these resources to God, but they have a respect for nature. Here's an opening for us to share our story of how the world came into existence and how the evil we see around us soon will come to an end."

- **Share the blessing.** HappyHand Copenhagen has been such a success that an-other HappyHand store has started in Aalborg, Denmark's fourth largest city. "We hope that the HappyHand concept will expand and become global," says Berit. "No church in the whole world should be without a HappyHand. It's such an ef-fective and blessed way to reach out to communities and to share God's love and compassion. It's a different way to open the doors of our churches, inviting people into our fellowship and at the same time showing them that we want to help people in need."

was established to bury the dead; HappyHand was established to represent the One who is the resurrection and the life.

HappyHand is a nonprofit second-hand shop—a thrift store—selling clothes, furniture, and household items. Its name refers to "lending a hand" to the community and the joy that engagement in mission brings. "In HappyHand we hold an important value—'pass it on,' " says Anne-May Müller, a regular volunteer at the store and Family Ministries director for the Danish Union of Seventh-day Adventists. "It's our aim to pass on the gifts we've received from God—both on a physical and spiritual level."

HappyHand was founded and continues to be managed by Berit Elkjær, a dynamic woman with a large vision and a passion for mission. "I love Jesus as my friend," she says. "He inspires us to share with other people." While running her own business, Berit has also held positions in her local church, volunteered in various ministry projects, and currently serves on the Trans-European Division and Danish Union executive committees.

HappyHand is her spiritual baby. "It's such an effective and blessed way to reach out to the community and share God's love and compassion," she says. "It's a different way to open the doors of our churches, inviting people into our fellowship, and at the same time showing them that we want to help people in need."

Thomas Müller, president of the Seventh-day Adventist Church in Denmark, confesses that he initially didn't realize the potential of HappyHand as a Center of Influence. "I've personally been encouraged, and I must admit, surprised," he says. "HappyHand has given us a platform to share our faith. We've spent thousands of hours distributing tracts and literature in order to get the attention of people around us. Suddenly we have people coming to us on our turf asking who we are, what we believe, and why we are doing this. This is the best part of the shop."

People passing by 58 Nørrebrogade are greeted by cheerful HappyHand signage and a large window showcasing the range of products for sale. As they step inside, they discover a calm atmosphere a world away from the bustling street outside. They're not stepping into a church, but many comment on the peaceful feeling they experience inside. This hasn't happened by accident—HappyHand is a Center of Influence that is much prayed for.

"Even though people are shopping, they still feel the warmth of the place," says Anita Thortzen, a young Adventist volunteer who cares for the store's Web site, social media, and event invitations. A prayer table sits at the back of the store, where customers can write prayer requests and place them in a prayer box. They can also take home small stickers with Bible promises. Anne-May has made friends through the store who now come to visit because they want someone to talk with and because they want prayer. "At first we were skeptical how customers would respond," she says, "but God always proves the skeptics wrong. We get a lot of prayer requests every week. And we've found that when people are standing by that table, they're more open to conversations."

FOR THE LEAST OF THESE

Berit Elkjær has a particular heart for the "least of these." "Jesus was there for the weak and outcasts, the poor and hungry," she says. "We, too, need to be there for them." She refers to Ellen White's statement:

> Those who stand as reformers, bearing the banner of the third angel's message, are the ones who are to draw out the soul to the hungry, and satisfy the afflicted soul. They are to do the work of Christ with hearts full of compassion for the widow and the orphan. But how strangely has this work been neglected! Other denominations have provided homes for the homeless; why were we not, years ago, planning to care for these needy ones whom Christ has committed to us, and whom he declares to be representatives of himself? Why have our people been so slow to hear the earnest appeals for help? The grief and affliction of the widow and orphan should be our grief (Ellen White, *The Home Missionary*, July 1, 1891).

During the colder months, HappyHand runs a ministry to the homeless, which Anne-May describes as "a project close to our hearts." She adds: "Although few actually sleep on the streets of Copenhagen because of shelters available, they still have no home, no money—and most of them have extremely messed up, tough lives. We have to love them too—and we do."

Anita Thortzen considers this ministry one of the highlights of volunteering with Happy-Hand. "Having a real, genuine smile from these people who are living some really rough lives gives me a warm feeling inside and makes it all feel very meaningful," she says.

Each weekend, volunteers meet at the store to pack fresh fruit and take it to the Adventist Development and Relief Agency (ADRA) van, which is full of warm clothes and toiletries. They first visit a shelter for women—mainly drug addicts and prostitutes. Then they visit a men's shelter. "They get a warm drink, some clothes, a bag of fruit, a smile—maybe even a hug," says Anne-May. "And they also get the knowledge that someone out in this cold world cares about them."

HappyHand donates most of its profits to humanitarian projects locally and internationally. Through the Adventist Development and Relief Agency (ADRA), Happy-Hand has supported projects such as refugee homes and drilling wells in Africa, as well as caring for the poor and needy in Copenhagen itself. "We ought not to fail in showing God's love in a practical way," adds Berit. "Our faith gives meaning when it results in practical love."

It was natural to be skeptical. Denmark's official Web site states: "Denmark is . . . among the world's most secularized countries, in which religion and Christianity play only a minor, often indirect, role in public life." And yet, as Thomas Müller points out, the average Dane is open toward spiritual questions. "But," he adds, "this is still a very private issue that is not discussed with others." This is why Christ's method of ministry, followed in HappyHand, is so important. "We need to gain people's confidence and respect before anyone is open to listen," he says. "As Adventist Christians, we simply have not earned the right to speak about spiritual topics before we have befriended people. There is a high wall of suspicion that needs to be pulled down by simple friendship—showing people that we are interested in them as people, not just as 'subjects' needing conversion."

Space is made in HappyHand for customers to sit down, rest, and enjoy free refreshments. Gentle music plays in the background, and conversations naturally occur. At the rear of the store, a simple but elegantly decorated prayer room provides a space for pastors and volunteers to have a private moment with customers who wish to talk and have someone pray with them. Bible study groups for customers and non-church volunteers are held regularly—one led by a pastor, another by lay people. Every second Sabbath of the month, HappyHand hosts a "Bible brunch," where people study the Bible, pray, and eat together. Leaders see this as the early stages of establishing a new group of believers.

The store is also used in the evenings for various spiritual events. These have included concerts, a talk by an astronomer on the existence of God, a seminar on building stronger families and marriages, presentations on Creation, Spiritual Wellness evenings, and even a presentation on the truth about the spirit world. HappyHand also holds craft nights where, for example, people can come together and make unique handmade cards to sell in the shop, or create decorations at Christmastime.

At any given time you may see, side by side in the store, the rich who support the ecologically sound principle of recycling and the poor who support the pragmatically sound principle of buying something cheaply. You may find elderly Danes beside newly arrived immigrants from Pakistan or Bosnia or Somalia or the Middle East. You may find young and old, believers and atheists. Volunteers staff the store. Thirty percent of the staff don't belong to the Adventist Church—"They just show up on our doorstep and ask, 'Can I help?' " says Anne-May. She adds, "It's a joy to share our faith in Jesus with them in very practical ways."

"I think it's a very practical way of being a Christian," adds Anita. "I can actually see the help we're giving. We meet people here, and it actually makes a difference." The ability to make contact with people, talk with people, and do something for them appeals to her. "Just having a second-hand shop wouldn't be enough for me, because there are lots of those," she says. "But having this extra [spiritual] aspect really makes it worth it. It's very public that this is a Christian shop. We have Bible verses on the walls, and it's very open and easy to get into conversations with people."

PASTOR'S DAY AT HAPPYHAND

One day a week, a sign out the front of HappyHand alerts people that a pastor is available in the store to talk or pray with people. "I like this way of being a pastor," says Anette Wulf, who spends Pastor's Day helping stock shelves, sort clothes, and talking and praying with people. Anette came from a strong atheist family but became a Christian at age 24 through the influence of a friend. A friend recalls Anette looking at her as if she were weird whenever she talked of God. But over time Anette decided to look more closely at faith and had a life-changing encounter with God. She started attending an Adventist café church in Copenhagen and then decided to study theology. "I'm a good example of how I think people come to God now," she says. "Most of the time it's through relationships that people come to God and get to know Him."

Anette tells of a homeless man who came into the store one day and wanted to talk. He told her he had been homeless on and off for many years. Finally the authorities had helped him get an apartment and paid most of it. But he was responsible for paying the rest, and if he couldn't find the money he would miss out on the apartment. He asked if HappyHand could help him apply for help from a foundation that sometimes helps homeless people. They helped him with the application, but Anette and some others were concerned that he might still miss out on the apartment. So they approached the HappyHand board and asked if they could lend him the money, or simply give it to him.

"We don't normally do things like that, because we can't lend money to all the homeless people," says Anette. "But we decided to help this one time. We also found household items from the shop that he needed. So he got his apartment and is now trying to start a new life." The man doesn't believe in God, but he comes to the shop regularly, sits and talks, and even allows staff to pray for him. He now has a place to live and receives a regular pension from the government. "Now we hope and pray that he will get to know Jesus," says Anette. "And we think that's possible because we keep listening, talking, and showing him the love of God."

You can see photos of the HappyHand store on its Danish-language Web site at www.happy-hand.dk.

"Anybody can be useful," adds Berit, "talking to people, decorating the shop windows, taking care of business, serving customers, making donated clothes ready for sale, starting Bible study groups, coordinating debate evenings or helping with projects for the homeless. God has a task for everyone, and He wants to change the world! And with God's help, HappyHand changes the world!"

Berit recalls their first customer—a five-year-old boy who visited the store with his mother. They started visiting regularly, and after a while the mother volunteered to help with the store. Tragically, the little boy became ill and died. "It was unbearable for all of us," says Berit. "I wanted so much to talk to her about life after death, about a loving God who one day will make all things new." One day the boy's mother and Berit were working together in the store, when suddenly the opportunity arose. She talked with the woman about sin, evil, and death—and how in the middle of all that there is a loving God who will one day create a new heaven and a new earth. "To see a mother's broken heart lighten up with hope is so touching," Berit recalls. "To watch the first, hesitating steps toward faith in God—that makes sense!"

It also makes sense that HappyHand leaders hope to see other stores established around the world. Berit challenges church members: "Go ahead with a HappyHand project in your town or city. God has a task for everyone, and He wants to change the world. And with God's help, HappyHand changes the world!"

MINISTERING TO NEEDS

"THE SAVIOR MINGLED WITH MEN AS ONE WHO DESIRED THEIR GOOD. HE SHOWED HIS SYMPATHY FOR THEM, *MINISTERED TO THEIR NEEDS.*"

ELLEN G. WHITE

"JESUS MINISTERED TO NEEDS AND ALWAYS LOOKED FOR WAYS to work with what people already had in place. For example, when He fed the famished multitudes, He used the community's available assets: bread and fish. Often when we are confronted with the needs in our communities, we fail to see what assets and tools they already have in place, and instead we look to provide solutions from outside the community. But we must honor our neighbors, their stories, and their knowledge. We thereby recognize that even in the midst of plight, the solution is often staring us right in the face."

Stevan Mirkovich has served as an urban church planter and currently pastors the Cornerstone Seventh-day Adventist Church in Vancouver, Canada.

"YOUNG PEOPLE IN KINSHASA HAVE BEEN DISTRIBUTING BOOKS, visiting door to door, and serving old people by drawing water, finding them firewood, and collecting clothes to give them from local churches."

Ambroise Fumakwa is president of the West Congo Union Mission, based in Kinshasa, Democratic Republic of Congo.

"HEALTH MINISTRY IS AN ENTRY POINT to reach urban people. It allows us to mingle, show sympathy, and minister to needs. Jesus used health ministry to attract people's attention, win their confidence, and then bid people to follow Him. It's an essential element in fulfilling Christ's method of comprehensive evangelism."

Rusli Heince was the leader of the Chinese ministry in the city of Jakarta, Indonesia, and currently is studying at the Adventist International Institute of Advanced Studies (AIIAS).

"SOME PEOPLE WHO MIGHT OTHERWISE BE HOSTILE to the message of Jesus Christ become open to it when their felt needs are addressed and met. As part of the 'Mission to the City' initiative in New York City, churches organized soup kitchens, hot meals, a food pantry, and a health van ministry. Pathfinders and young people organized compassion rallies—going out into the community to do acts of kindness, distribute gifts, and clean up the streets.

"Ministering to needs helped bridge the gap between church and community as both came together to effect positive changes. Panels of pastors, community leaders, teachers, and police officers discussed social concerns. There were also special prayer sessions for the mayor of the city, police officers, and civic leaders.

"Urban areas are full of strangers, estranged from their own past, culture, and countries of origin. These examples of ministering to needs show how we can help bridge what is often viewed as a hostile space between community and church."

Alanzo Smith is ministerial director and family ministries director for the Greater New York Conference and has extensive experience pastoring in urban areas.

CHAPTER 6

A WAY TO THE HEART OF THE CITY

*A spiritual odyssey leads to a
health-based model of urban outreach.*

BETTINA KRAUSE[1]

*O*NE FAMILY FOLLOWED GOD'S CALL *to retreat from the city. To their surprise, He then gave them a mission to return and pioneer a ministry that's focused on building trust and meeting the needs of busy Russian urbanites who have little interest in the Advent message.*

TVER, RUSSIAN FEDERATION

If you make the nine-hour car journey from Moscow to St. Petersburg on Russia's M10 highway, you'll drive past the city of Tver, just 150 kilometers north of Moscow. This city of almost half a million people spreads out from the banks of the leisurely flowing Volga and Tvertsa rivers, which converge here. Eighteenth- and nineteenth-century buildings mix with Soviet-era architecture, and the streets of this thriving administrative center are busy with traffic and pedestrians. If you follow the signs to the city center and drive along one of its main thoroughfares, you may come across a small shop, surrounded by office buildings, with a sign displaying its name: Garden of Eden.

More than one thousand people each month—many of them workers from the nearby offices—open the door to the Garden of Eden and walk inside. They may be looking for information about improving their diet or searching for some natural remedies. They may just want to browse the shelves of vegetarian food and diabetic products or look through the store's selection of books.

This downtown Garden of Eden store is one of two healthful living shops in Tver that are operated by members of the nearby Emmaus Seventh-day Adventist Church.

---

1   A special Thank You to Galina Stele and Victor Kozacov for their invaluable assistance with this chapter, and to Victoria Nikulina for her translations.

In the words of Valeri Zhinov'ev, leader of the Garden of Eden project, each store is a "lighthouse" of hope in this difficult urban mission field.

TRUE LIBERTY

The city of Tver holds a fascinating place in Russia's rich literary heritage. More than 200 years ago, author Alexander Radischev wrote *A Journey from Petersburg to Moscow,* a book that traced an imaginary journey between these two cities. Radischev presented various stories—allegories—set in the towns and villages along the route to Moscow, and he devoted one chapter to Tver. His goal? To expose the political corruption and social ills he saw within contemporary Russian society. Radischev's book catapulted him to fame, but it was probably not the kind of attention he wanted. Catherine the Great, the reigning empress of Russia, had Radischev arrested for treason, and he was sentenced to death, a punishment that was later lightened to eight years' exile in Siberia.

Catherine was correct in sensing the potentially revolutionary impact of Radischev's book. In the chapter set in the city of Tver, Radischev includes an "Ode to Liberty," which through the years has inspired generations of revolutionaries, not just in Russia but in many other countries as well.

Today in Tver and across Russia, people still have the same age-old desire for a life of purpose and fulfillment, according to Victor Kozakov, Adventist Mission director for the Adventist Church in the Euro-Asia Division. And yet sharing Christ's ultimate gift of liberty—freedom from sin and hopelessness—is not easy in the urban centers of Russia.

"In many Russian cities, people are quite secular, and they don't show any particular interest in spiritual issues," says Kozakov. Paradoxically, many *also* consider themselves to be Russian Orthodox believers—a label that carries a vast cultural and historical weight for most Russians. It's the faith of their parents, the faith of their nation, and it's an integral part of their self-identity as Russians.

And yet, for the vast majority, their faith is nominal. "They know very little or nothing about Christianity," says Kozakov.

A related challenge is the Adventist Church's often negative public image. If the church is thought of at all by ordinary Russians, it's as a "foreign sect"—an unknown, unfamiliar organization that one would probably do well to avoid.

This alone can be a formidable barrier for any form of urban ministry, explains Kozakov.

Kozakov also identifies more practical challenges. The availability of vast quantities of information online or on television means that Russians are now far less likely to leave their homes of an evening to attend health lectures or meetings that, in times past, have been such a key element of traditional evangelistic methods. As Kozakov points out, why should people go to so much effort to seek information when they have many more electronic resources at their fingertips?

A PERSONAL SPIRITUAL QUEST

These are some of the daunting obstacles to mission that Adventist Church member Valeri Zhinov'ev has often pondered. Prior to 2012, Valeri, his wife and their three children lived in Tver, and he describes their life then as similar to any "average church member."

"Work, family, Sabbath. But my heart was not fully satisfied, there was a feeling of emptiness," he says.

Valeri, a successful businessman, felt pressured to be always on the move, to "catch up to something," yet when he achieved each goal he felt no satisfaction. There was always a new goal to chase, and so the cycle continued.

Ironically, Valeri's path toward urban mission work began when he and his wife decided to move *out* of the city. In 2011, they began to study Ellen White's writings and other spiritual books, which strengthened their long-held desire to move from Tver into the nearby countryside. They were motivated by the hope that they could break the pattern of endless goal-chasing, spend more time in nature, and experience more fully a sense of the Lord's presence. They teamed up with some fellow church members and searched for a piece of land, finally purchasing 40 hectares of property on the banks of the Orsha River, about 20 kilometers from Tver.

But Valeri was still searching for God's purpose for him. For a short time, he and his wife attended a medical missionary school in Novye Obihody in Ukraine, and on returning to Tver they decided to leave secular employment and dedicate their lives to ministry. In 2013, they returned to Obihody with their three children for a six-month program.

Here, everything changed for Valeri and his family. He developed friendships with many people who, in his words, "don't live by the principles of this world"—whose goals don't include buying an apartment or owning a car and mobile phone.

"I don't mean that we don't need this, but it all has very little value in the end," says Valeri. "However, if you start to live instead for others' happiness, it will give you indescribable joy."

SPIRITUAL REVIVAL—FOR MISSION

On returning to their home outside Tver, Valeri and his family continued to pray and ask for God's guidance. They came up with the idea of holding a camp meeting on their property as a way of seeking spiritual revival for the church in the Tver area.

"It's important, like the people of Israel during the Feast of the Tabernacles, to leave our work and gather in nature for a few days to listen to spiritual instruction and think about our life and ministry." At this gathering they met someone who invited them to a meeting in Krasny Mak in the Crimean mountains to learn about "health food ministry." They went, even though they thought it might be a waste of time.

But it was here that Valeri and his wife first began to understand that the Lord had called them out of the city to prepare them for a special mission—one that would take them right back to where they began.

IS IT REALLY A MINISTRY?

When new mission models are misunderstood

One of the most significant benefits so far of the Garden of Eden project in Tver is the engagement of church members in hands-on mission work. With just 45 baptized members, the Emmaus church is supporting two Garden of Eden stores in the city, and this requires a tremendous amount of work and dedication, day after day, week after week.

"This is a very blessed ministry, and people need it," says Valeri Zhinov'ev. But not all Adventist members in the surrounding area are equally supportive or understand that the stores' primary purpose is to share the gospel, not make sales.

"They think if we deal with money and sell food, we are businessmen," says Valeri. "If the whole church, I mean all members, in our city of Tver would become involved in the ministry, we could organize health clubs, cooking classes, and more. But we don't have enough people for it or enough time.

"We are trying to explain to all members the importance of this ministry," he adds. Nikolai G. Chekh, general manager of the newly opened health food store in St. Petersburg, explained their approach to urban outreach in a recent interview with ESD News. "The way to the Lord does not always go through the house of prayer," he said. "Sometimes it is not easy for a person to cross its threshold. We believe that through our good attitude, people will express a desire to learn about God. Our first priority is a non-commercial one, but we want to . . . find a way to the heart of people through social service."

In Krasny Mak, Valeri met Alexey and Veronica Lubsky, a family from the town of Pyatigorsk, located more than 1,700 kilometers (1,050 miles) from Tver in the mountainous Caucasus region of southern Russia. Alexey and Veronica had opened a health store in Pyatigorsk a few years earlier. "Would you help us if we decided to open a store in Tver?" asked Valeri. The couple agreed, and the Garden of Eden project was born. Valeri's first step was to take his idea to the leaders of his local congregation near Tver, the Emmaus Adventist church.

The Emmaus church, established in 1997, is a growing, active congregation. When church pastor Stanislav Petrovich Bazilo arrived in 2011, there were 15 members. Today, the church has a membership of 45, but about 60 people attend worship each Sabbath morning. "We also have many children in our congregation," says Bazilo. "We don't have enough space in our church building."

Bazilo describes his church members as very missionary minded. The members organize the distribution of an Adventist newspaper to surrounding towns and villages, and the church's Pathfinder club takes on various outreach projects, such as health exhibitions or community cleanup days.

But until Valeri came to them with his idea for a health food store, the church lacked any permanent ministry presence in the nearby city of Tver.

The Emmaus church was immediately supportive of Valeri's plan—in fact, the entire congregation voted to officially adopt the ministry.

FINDING GOD'S PLAN

The first hurdle was locating suitable premises—not a simple proposition given the tight budget and the need to be in a central, and thus more expensive, location.

A frustrating search followed. "All that was offered to us was very expensive or wasn't the right size," recalls Valeri. One morning during worship, Valeri was reading from Proverbs and was struck by the counsel in chapter 24, verse 6: "Surely you need guidance to wage war, and victory is won through many advisers" (NIV).

He spoke first to a church elder, who advised Valeri to adjust his plans and accept a smaller store space, but Valeri found the idea of downsizing his dream difficult to accept. Later that day, Alexey from Pyatigorsk called Valeri to see how the search for a premises was going. He, too, suggested Valeri find a smaller, less expensive place to rent.

"I realized that the Lord had talked to me through two people, telling me the same thing," says Valeri.

Still, Valeri talked to one more person—someone who had promised to support the ministry financially. This man pointed Valeri to Ellen White's counsel that sometimes ministries need to start small.

The next day, Valeri was shown premises on a main street near the center of town in an area with office buildings and near a Russian Orthodox chapel. It was a small space but well located, and Valeri did not have to think long before signing a rental agreement.

Immediately, the Emmaus congregation moved into action, helping fit out the shop with Russian-style wooden shelves and counters, sourcing products and negotiating supply contracts, helping sew aprons for shop servers, and filling shelves with goods. Even Valeri's children helped by packing products and sticking on labels and Bible verses. Valeri's friends, Alexey and Veronica, made the 20-hour car trip from Pyatigorsk, their car filled to overflowing with products from their own health store. Within a week, the Garden of Eden store was ready to open its doors.

"AFRAID" OF ADVENTISTS NO MORE

The store has been operating for only a short time—it opened on October 26, 2014—but already it is making its presence felt in the community.

"We have good communication with the people who come into the store, and distribute many Adventist newspapers and books," says Valeri. "Many people come into the store just to take a newspaper or to talk."

"I can see that many people, as they get to know our shop assistants, are not afraid of the word *Adventist* anymore," adds Valeri. "They see that we are not fanatic but that we understand their needs.

"These people become more open when they realize we're not trying just to sell something or tell them about our doctrines, but we care about them."

Valeri says that the time will come when it's right to invite them to church, but not yet.

For now, he says, "they are not afraid to come to talk to us." A seemingly small thing, but, in the context of urban mission in Russia, it's a momentous step forward.

A NEEDS-FOCUSED MINISTRY

Within just a few months, the Emmaus church opened a second Garden of Eden store in Tver, this one in a residential district, and a church elder, Sergei Kirillov, became its manager. The second store attracts a different type of customer—mainly workers and pensioners who enjoy coming by to talk or browse the shelves. On average, between 800 and 1,400 people visit each store every month.

The Russian Orthodox chapel near the original Garden of Eden store has also become an unexpected source of customers. The Orthodox tradition calls for fasts on certain weekdays and throughout the liturgical calendar, when eating meat, fish, dairy, and eggs is forbidden. Valeri says that some people from the Orthodox fellowship came to the store and decided to advertise the store among their members. They went even further, entering details about the Garden of Eden in a local information service for the wider community.

Since beginning this ministry, Valeri and his team have been constantly learning and adapting.

"One day a woman wanted to buy a book in our store but couldn't afford it," says Valeri. "The next day, two brothers from our church, who have their own businesses, came to the store and asked us how the book selling was going." Valeri explained the problem—it wasn't that customers weren't interested, but many simply didn't have an income that allowed them to buy many books.

The two businessmen came up with a solution. They offered to provide money to cover most of the books' cost, allowing the store to offer the books at a vastly reduced price.

Valeri has noticed, also, that many customers treat the store like a pharmacy and come in simply to get diet or remedy advice from the sales assistants. He says that if they could open an associated health room, it would spark a "revolution in the ministry." Even further down the track, he sees the possibility of opening a vegetarian café.

Victor Kozakov, the Adventist Mission director, sees tremendous potential in the ministry that Valeri and the Emmaus church have started in Tver, as well as other similar ventures around the Division. Early in 2015, a healthy living store called The Fig Tree opened in St. Petersburg, with a second store set to open soon in a different district of the city.

"A healthy food store is a ministry that responds to people's needs," says Kozakov. He also says it builds on issues of growing interest for many people in Russian cities—good nutrition and building a healthy lifestyle. He points out that traditional means of offering this information, in seminars or special programs, has lost much appeal for city dwellers. But the opportunity to come and buy inexpensive, healthy food and to talk with knowledgeable sales assistants is intriguing for many people.

"Through such stores we not only give valuable information to people but we also show them how to apply these principles in real life," explains Kozakov. "When they talk with staff, customers see that these are not just regular food stores but that the staff are committed to giving practical help to every customer."

CREATING A NON-THREATENING SPACE FOR MISSION IN THE CITY
Lessons from the front lines of urban mission

- **Listen for God's leading.** Listen and follow, no matter where it takes you. Sometimes you need to retreat from the city to gain spiritual insights and strength for urban ministry.
- **Lean on fellow believers.** Depend on the knowledge and support of fellow believers who are also engaged in urban outreach. Through them, you can be inspired with new ideas and draw on a wealth of experience-based lessons for reaching the cities for Christ.
- **Engage local churches.** Sometimes, the crucial first step in an urban outreach project is engaging local Adventist churches. They are your invaluable partners in mission, but at first, some may need extra time to catch a vision for where the Holy Spirit is leading.
- **Learn and adapt as you go along.** Be prepared to let go of some of your assumptions about how your ministry should look. Trust the Lord to lead.

CHAPTER 7

"WE'RE NO LONGER THE SAME"

When God grows a ministry,
it's all about trying to keep up.

BETTINA KRAUSE[1]

*P*ARADISE VALLEY SEVENTH-DAY ADVENTIST CHURCH *was a shrinking inner-city congregation that seemed destined for irrelevance. One day, it dared to ask, "Why are we here? What's our purpose?" And then everything began to change.*

SAN DIEGO, CALIFORNIA, UNITED STATES

Every person sitting in the English language school at Paradise Valley Adventist Community Center has a story of loss. They're refugees—from Congo, Rwanda, Iraq, Afghanistan, Bhutan, and many others places. At the very least, they've left behind their language and culture, but many have also lost parents, siblings, or children. Driven by civil war or political violence, they've abandoned homes, professions and everything familiar, and now they're adrift in a world where even the simplest transaction—from enrolling their children in school to dealing with government agencies—can be an exercise in confusion. They've come to San Diego with their lives, their dignity, a sense of hope, but little else.

There's 35-year-old Vanessa Mobole, born in the Democratic Republic of Congo, who was with her father when he was murdered in 2004 by Rwandan rebel forces. She escaped from the house, hiding with friends and eventually making her way to the United States, via Burundi and Uganda.

Or there's Jean-Marie Katula, a high school mathematics teacher and human rights activist, also from the Congo, whose first wife was murdered by government militia and whose outspokenness has landed him in jail in both Congo and Rwanda.

---

1 Special thanks to Jocelyn Fay from Paradise Valley church, who provided stories, information, and invaluable assistance.

Then there's a whole contingent of men and women from countries in Southeast Asia—Bhutan, Laos, Nepal, Cambodia, Vietnam—many of whom fled ethnic or political violence and spent years in Thai or Nepalese refugee camps before being granted asylum in the United States.

For hundreds of the almost 200,000 refugees living in San Diego, Paradise Valley Seventh-day Adventist Church and its Refugee Assimilation Project has become a lifeline—physically and emotionally—in their effort to restart their interrupted lives.

Almost every weekday, trucks from Paradise Valley church do the rounds of food banks and stores such as Walmart and Target, picking up food donations. Once a week, a truck visits nearby apartment complexes delivering food, along with clothing, diapers and other essentials. And every Tuesday, the church's Community Services Center hums with activity as some 11,000 pounds of food and hundreds of pieces of clothing are distributed to refugee families.

On weekdays, a church bus also makes its way through the streets of San Diego picking up men and women for English language classes at the church's community center. As the students arrive, the room fills with a low hum of many different languages—Arabic, French, Nepalese, and Spanish.

A nearby thrift store, operated by Paradise Valley Adventist church, has a constant stream of customers. The store serves a dual purpose—not only does it offer refugee families low cost clothes and household goods, but students from the language school can also gain valuable work experience.

In terraced gardens near the church, men and women chat and sing as they work in garden plots. The project provides the chance for families to grow fresh food, and it's also an antidote to the anxiety and depression experienced by many refugees.

Each Sabbath morning, the three Paradise Valley church buses again move through city streets, picking up worshippers for Sabbath School and church. Families representing some 50 different nationalities and ethnicities sit together in the pews. Sabbath Schools are conducted in French, Laotian, Spanish, Tagalog, Swahili, Kinyarwanda, Nepalese, as well as English. During the church service, translation is offered over FM headsets in Arabic, Laotian, Nepalese, French, and Spanish.

A CHURCH TRANSFORMED

Paradise Valley church and its refugee ministry has spawned hundreds of stories of personal transformation—men and women who've gained not just a firmer foothold in their new homeland but also a much-needed sense of acceptance and belonging. In many instances, they've found a spiritual home as well—as senior pastor Will James says: "Our baptismal font is rarely dry." In the past seven years, more than 250 people have joined the church through baptism.

But perhaps the most remarkable story of transformation belongs to the congregation itself. Over the past 10 years, Paradise Valley church has experienced nothing less than a revolution in its mission focus and its impact in the community.

To really understand the extraordinary metamorphosis of this congregation, you have to go back more than a century to 1904, when Adventist Church leader Ellen White visited San Diego. She saw a vacant, somewhat dilapidated sanitarium building and became convinced that the Lord wanted the Adventist Church to establish a health work there. But there was just one small problem—there was no water supply. In fact, the sanitarium had fallen into disuse because of a drought in the area and the lack of an artesian well on the property. Nevertheless, Mrs. White personally put $2,000 toward the purchase of the sanitarium.

An Adventist well-digger was employed to find a water source, but after digging to a depth of 80 feet without success, he was discouraged. He went to Ellen White and asked whether she was sure the Lord had led her to the Paradise Valley property. She affirmed that He had. "All right," he said, "the Lord would not give us an elephant without providing water for it to drink."[2] He continued on, and at last he struck a stream of water "as large as a man's arm." The well he sank in 1904 still gives water today.

The Paradise Valley Sanitarium was an immediate success, and through the decades it continued to expand its services and capacity. By 2004, it was a hospital with 210 patient beds, a 24-hour emergency room, a well-equipped surgery suite, and a range of other health services.

Just down the road, the Paradise Valley Adventist church grew alongside the hospital, drawing its membership and identity largely from its successful next-door neighbor. Will, who came as senior pastor in 2004, describes the church he first encountered as "comfortable, but somewhat complacent." The ethnic make-up of the congregation was largely Caucasian and Filipino—not a true demographic reflection of its south San Diego location. Nor did the church membership mirror local economic realities. Household incomes in the area around the church are well below the state average.

It was mainly an "observer" church, says Will. The majority of members came each week, sat in the pews, and watched the worship service. They sang hymns and went home—not necessarily because they lacked a heart for mission, but because they were never called on to use their spiritual gifts.

But then came a twist in the story of Paradise Valley church. The nearby hospital had been battling a growing deficit for many years, and by the mid-2000s, its shaky finances had worsened. On March 1, 2007, Adventist Health formally announced the sale of the hospital.

The decision shocked the Adventist community in San Diego and the Paradise Valley congregation in particular. For this proud institutional church, the move seemed to foreshadow the beginning of a long, slow slide into irrelevance. The pews became more sparsely occupied, and the church's glory days seemed well in the past. The large sanctuary and spacious church facilities—indirect products of the well-digger's "thirsty elephant"—were fast becoming white elephants.

---

2 Wayne R. Judd and Jonathan M. Butler, eds., *Thirsty Elephant: The Story of Paradise Valley Hospital* (Riverside, CA: La Sierra University Press, 1994).

The Holy Spirit, however, had other plans. In hindsight, Will sees this period of uncertainty as the time when members of his congregation finally began to transition from observers to activists.

MORE THAN A SOCIAL CLUB

When you talk with Will, it's soon clear that he has an aversion to clubs that masquerade as churches. He believes a club mentality—caring mainly for members' needs—results in an inward focus that alienates a church from the community in which it's located.

"Almost every week in my sermon, I try to make the point that the church has to have a reason for being, beyond just looking after ourselves," he says. "The church isn't a social club. I tell my congregation that God has called and ordained each one of us as a minister. We're here for a purpose; we need to find our gifts. And when we find our purpose, we need to fulfill it!"

Even before the sale of Paradise Valley Hospital, Will and his wife, Peggy, had begun an effort to revitalize the church's community services program. For many years, the church's community center, a 1,400-square-meter (15,000-square-foot) facility built in the 1960s, had hosted quilting bees and small-scale programs such as distributing clothing and bread. Peggy, who became community services director in 2004, began to look for ways to expand the range of community services the church offered.

Soon afterward, says Will, God started opening doors. It began with a visit from a Laotian man—formerly a Buddhist monk—who had accepted Christ and been baptized as an Adventist church member while living in a Thai refugee camp. He was eventually granted asylum in the United States and settled in San Diego, and before long, he'd started a small home-based outreach ministry to other Laotian refugees.

Will recalls, "He came to me one day and asked, 'Do you think your church could love and accept us? We need a church home.' And I said, 'Of course!' So this small group of Laotians started attending Paradise Valley church."

Every week, the former monk delivered food parcels from the church to Laotian refugees in a nearby apartment complex. A group of Bhutanese refugees living in the same building began to notice this man with his bags of food, and one day they asked him to bring them food as well. So he did. Before long, the Bhutanese refugees were curious about the church that provided these packages, and many of them began to attend church each Sabbath.

"We didn't speak Bhutanese—or Nepalese, which many of them spoke—but we loved them!" says Will. "We borrowed a bus from a Sunday church and began to pick them up on Sabbath morning. We bought them all Nepalese Bibles, and they were delighted to have them, but we immediately notice they held them upside down. They were illiterate, even in their mother tongue."

This was a turning point for members of the community services team at Paradise Valley Church. They asked, "What can we do to *really* help these refugees? What

BUILDING A PRACTICAL, PEOPLE-FOCUSED MINISTRY

Lessons from the front lines of urban mission

- **Find your purpose.** God has placed you where you are for a unique reason—find out what that is.
- **Be prepared to change.** Allow God to transform the status quo, and trust where He takes you.
- **Customize your mission.** Don't simply try to emulate another church's ministry. Your ministry has to fit both the needs of your local community and the gifts within your congregation.
- **Be real.** Genuine impact happens when a church strives to meet real community needs—not imagined or assumed needs. Analyze your neighborhood.
- **Be practical.** Traditional public evangelism doesn't work in your urban community? Then let the Holy Spirit work through "practical evangelism" as you seek to reveal the character of Christ in your neighborhood.
- **Be people focused.** Focus on forging authentic, long-term relationships, and offer assistance and friendship without strings attached. And then always keep the door of your church wide open.
- **Be prayer focused.** There *will* be challenges and setbacks, but prayer—both corporate and individual—is a powerful antidote to both.

You can find out more about Paradise Valley church's ever-expanding ministry at www.friendshipsforhope.org.

would make a significant difference in their lives?" And with that, the idea was born for an English language school for refugees.

A SNOWBALLING MINISTRY

Soon a pattern was established. As the members of Paradise Valley church responded to a particular need within the local refugee community, God wasted no time in presenting them with another need to be met; then another and another. And so Paradise Valley church's refugee ministry began to grow organically.

As God revealed needs, He also led the church to find resources in unexpected places. The recession of 2008 hit hard in inner-city San Diego, and Will realized the church needed to dramatically expand its capacity to store and distribute food. He placed an advertisement on Craigslist explaining the church's need for a large, walk-in cooler. A company that installed commercial coolers responded, offering to break down, move, and reassemble any cooler for them, free of charge. Soon after, a florist called. The store was going out of business and was happy to give Paradise

Valley church its cooler. The church also found money to buy a pickup truck for food deliveries and began a regular Tuesday program at the church for sorting and bagging supplies to be distributed.

Around this time, Ephraim Bendatunguka, an Adventist pastor from Rwanda who had been living and studying in Germany, moved to San Diego with his wife and four children. As they struggled to find their feet in the United States, Paradise Valley church cared for their needs, and before long, Pastor Bendatunguka was spearheading outreach among the many refugees from the Congo, Rwanda, and other African countries. Today, he still serves as director of the church's Refugee Assimilation Project.

Starting the English language school required a whole new level of coordination and funding. First, the church had to scrape together some $40,000 to purchase 20 laptops and 40 licenses to English language learning software. Next, it set up a school in the community center and sought out volunteer teachers to keep the school professionally staffed for five days a week.

The opening of the school was scheduled for September 1, 2011, but with just days to go, the church encountered a roadblock. "We discovered that for the refugees to receive food stamps, housing allowance, and medical insurance from the government, they needed to spend a minimum of 35 hours a week split between English language classes and work experience," explains Will. "So if we really wanted to minister to the refugee community, we needed to not only teach English but to provide work experience."

What first appeared to be a setback actually spurred a new ministry. Within a month, the church had leased a storefront space nearby and opened a thrift store as a means of providing work skills for its English language students. The store was soon thriving.

As the English language school quickly filled to capacity, God continued to prod Paradise Valley church in unexpected directions. Church volunteers working among refugee families discovered that depression was a pervasive and destructive force within this community.

"Sometimes we would see someone sitting in a fetal position, their head in their hands," says Will. Some refugees were overcome by their loss and their sense of alienation; the feeling of being "strangers in a strange land."

"Ellen White talks about how healing it can be to get your hands in the soil and work in a garden," he says. "So we decided to start a community garden for the refugees."

The new non-Adventist owners of Paradise Valley Hospital leased the church some unused land for just $1, and soon the ground had been transformed into a patchwork of individual garden plots. The garden proved immensely popular. Not only could refugees grow some favorite crops from their homeland but they were also getting out of their often cramped apartments and connecting with other people.

CHRIST SAID, "FOLLOW ME"

For the past 12 years, Paradise Valley Seventh-day Adventist Church hasn't conducted any public evangelism campaigns. Instead, it has focused all its energy and resources on building relationships within the immediate community—all within a radius of just a few miles of the church building.

The church's approach to sharing Christ is low key, but as Will says, "It's working for us." Over the past year alone, some 50 people were baptized at the Paradise Valley church.

"We don't push baptisms," he says, "but the subject naturally comes up as people get to know us, see the church, and see what's going on here. They say, 'I want to be part of this! What do I have to do?'

"We're constantly rubbing shoulders with people in the community," adds Will. "Sometimes we'll ask someone whether they have a church family. If they don't, we say, 'We'd like to be your church family!' " He says it's a rare Sabbath morning that there isn't a new family from the community visiting Paradise Valley church.

Today, the church is more crowded than it was before the Adventist hospital was sold. But there are key differences. One of the main changes is that the faces of those in the pews now reflect the demographics of this San Diego neighborhood. Paradise Valley church has become a truly multicultural congregation.

Another change experienced by Paradise Valley church—less visible, perhaps, but just as profound—is the number of those within the congregation who regularly volunteer time to keep the church's various ministries running. Almost 130 volunteers help coordinate and staff the English language school, the thrift store, the community garden, the food delivery program, as well as the massive twice-yearly rummage sales that raise vital funds. In his many years of ministry, says Will, he has never before seen such a commitment to community involvement as he sees in his current congregation.

For some, volunteering at Paradise Valley church has literally been a life-changing experience. Jocelyn Fay, a veteran communication professional within the Adventist Church in North America, first heard about plans for the Refugee Assimilation Project when her friend, Will, sent her a draft of his ideas to edit.

At the time, Jocelyn was communication director for the Southeastern California Conference, based in Riverside. Immediately, she was captivated by Will's plan and his vision to make Christ's compassion real in such practical ways within the Paradise Valley community.

"I edited the document and then sent it to a friend of mine on the east coast—a professional fundraiser—and asked her for ideas," says Jocelyn. She kept in touch with Will, and later, when Jocelyn retired, she chose to move from Riverside to Paradise Valley so she could volunteer with the project.

"I could have stayed in Riverside, I guess, and gone to the gym and met friends for lunch," she says, "But that would have been boring after a while. Here, it's never boring!" Most rewarding for Jocelyn has been the long-term relationships she has built with many of those who've participated in one or another of Paradise Valley's programs.

"We really adopt these people into our church family," says Jocelyn. "They may finish the language and work skills course, but they still come back to us for food or clothes or other things they need. We don't just push them out of the nest and say, 'See you later!' "

"THIS IS *OUR* PURPOSE"

Looking back, Will believes his congregation took its first step toward radical transformation when it really began to focus on the people who lived in the local community, and their needs.

This isn't as simple as it sounds, says Will. Too often, he says, it's easier to provide programs that we *think* people want. We project our own biases or assumptions, rather than finding out what people really need. According to Will, the only way to find out the needs of a community is to build friendships: to talk with people, to regularly go where people live, and to make an effort to understand them—their challenges and their dreams.

"The Lord convicted us that we needed to minister to our local refugee community," says Will. "It's not a ministry for every church, or even for every inner-city church. But it's *our* ministry. This is our purpose for being here, in this community."

He acknowledges that it hasn't been easy. "Challenging" is an understatement when it comes to describing the never-ending financial and personnel demands of the Refugee Assimilation Project. Keeping everything going is a logistical juggling act—coordinating volunteers, maintaining equipment, ensuring compliance with government regulations, and raising enough funds.

"God is the true center of our resources, though," says Will. "He will keep providing for our needs, so we can provide for the needs of others."

And then there are dreams of new ministries as God continues to open doors. In the short term, Paradise Valley church wants to expand its community garden and continue to grow its new childcare center for the children of refugees.

For the volunteers who care for the many different facets of the Refugee Assimilation Project, the work can be difficult and personally demanding. For leaders of the project, it has become an all-absorbing enterprise. So why do they continue? What motivates them? When asked, Will laughs. "That's easy," he says. "Love for God, and love for people. That's it. That's what drives us."

WINNING CONFIDENCE

"THE SAVIOR MINGLED WITH MEN
AS ONE WHO DESIRED THEIR GOOD.
HE SHOWED HIS SYMPATHY FOR THEM,
MINISTERED TO THEIR NEEDS, AND
WON THEIR CONFIDENCE."

ELLEN G. WHITE

"FOUR P'S FOR WINNING CONFIDENCE:
　　1. Provide temporal food
　　2. Pay attention to them
　　3. Provide spiritual food
　　4. Pray for them."

Ambassador of God *is a Global Mission pioneer (who prefers to stay anonymous), planting a church in the city of Bangkok, Thailand.*

"THERE ARE NO SHORTCUTS FOR THIS ONE! My practical tip: stay connected to people and share life with them. Confidence is built over time by being an intentional follower of Jesus who shares everyday life with people in the same ways Jesus did. You can't force people to trust you. It happens over time as we rub shoulders authentically and consistently with people in everyday situations. We gain confidence by listening, meeting needs, keeping our word, walking our talk, and by being there for people in good times and in challenging times."

Simon Martin *is a pastor and church planter in Dunstable, England.*

"WHAT HAPPENS WHEN WE MAKE PURPOSEFUL RELATIONSHIPS for the Kingdom? When we seek the best for people? When we demonstrate sympathy and serve people according to their needs? You're right: we make friends. True friendships, though, only come as the direct result of trust. This was the way Jesus broke down barriers of rejection and prejudice. This is the only way we will truly be able to show God's love for everyone.

However, we should always remember the importance of authenticity in our relationships. In urban and postmodern contexts we cannot simply 'forget' people if they don't respond according to our expectations. Trust is key! So, be authentic. Be real."

Kleber Gonçalves *is senior pastor of the Nova Semente Seventh-day Adventist Church in the heart of São Paulo, Brazil. He is also director of the Global Mission Center for Secular and Postmodern Studies.*

CHAPTER 8

A GOD-SIZED CHALLENGE

*Urban mission in China—making friends,
meeting needs, building trust.*

BETTINA KRAUSE[1]

*O*VER THE YEARS WE'VE HEARD FEW STORIES *about the work of Seventh-day Adventist Chinese nationals. And yet, silence does not mean inaction. What follows is a rare glimpse into the heart of one of the world's unique mission fields, as faithful Seventh-day Adventists take Christ's method into the streets and homes of China's rapidly changing urban landscape.*

AN UNNAMED CITY, CHINA

Two young Chinese Seventh-day Adventists kneel together in a small room. It's just a small room within a large apartment complex, within a vast city, within a country of some 1.4 billion men, women, and children—most of whom have little or no knowledge of Christianity.

These young Global Mission pioneers—church planters—pray, their words low and fervent. They are discouraged, close to breaking point. They came to this city full of plans to make friends, offer Bible studies, and begin a small group of believers in this place where there is no Seventh-day Adventist presence. It was a personal risk for them—China's residency laws don't allow individuals to move to another a city for mission work.

Over the months, they've worked hard, but no one has responded. There seems to be no way to reach the residents of this city, all apparently preoccupied with their work, their family, their lives.

"Dear heavenly Father," they pray, "Your children are very sad because there is no one for us to reach. If the situation keeps going on, then we will have to go home."

---

1 A special thanks goes to the Chinese Union Mission, and to Audrey Folkenberg for the stories in this chapter and for her invaluable assistance.

A few days later, they're packing up and getting ready to leave the city, their sense of failure weighing heavily on them. There's a knock at the door—it's a woman they've never seen before.

"Are you the people who've been handing out those religious tracts?" she demands.

"Yes," they reply, unsure of what she wants.

"I need to know the gospel," she replies simply.

And this is the answer to the young people's desperate prayer. It's a beginning, which leads to more interests, until, after some time, there are up to 15 people worshipping each Sabbath in the pioneers' small apartment, seven of them now baptized Seventh-day Adventists.

URBAN EVOLUTION

It's not an exaggeration to say that urban policy in China has suffered a severe case of whiplash in recent decades. In 1968, China's communist revolutionary leader, Chairman Mao Zedong, stepped up his efforts to drain the cities and move much of the Chinese population to the countryside.

"Let us not laze about in the cities," declared Mao in an influential newspaper article, published December 22, 1968, in the *People's Daily*. During the Cultural Revolution of the 1950s, cities were cast as wellsprings of dangerous values and ideas, which threatened communist ideals. Instead, said Mao, the Chinese people must be "educated from living in rural poverty."

Thus began one of the great internal migrations of the modern era. In 1969 alone, some two million educated young Chinese city-dwellers helped lead a "rustication movement"—a wave of millions of people leaving the cities and resettling in the rural provinces and villages of this vast nation, which covers a landmass of some 3.7 million square miles.

Today, China is again experiencing a massive internal migration—but this time in reverse. A recent *New York Times* series explored an unprecedented plan by the Chinese government to move some 250 million people from farms to cities over the next 12 to 15 years. It's a dramatic reversal in policy driven by economic realities, which are forcing China to retool its manufacturing and service sectors to better compete in the global marketplace.

Ghost cities—sprawling but, as yet, empty metropolises—are appearing where there were once farms and villages, products of an ambitious building program underway to accommodate China's new policy of urbanization.

This vast movement toward the cities in China builds on a trend that has been intensifying in recent years. Gradually, the government has been easing restrictions on city dwelling, prompting more and more people to leave their rural villages in search of the low-paying but stable employment offered in the factories of the cities. Projections suggest that by 2025, 70 percent of China's population will live in urban areas.

These incredible demographic shifts within China are bringing social upheaval in their wake. Some of these new city-dwellers face a sense of dislocation and alienation, a loss of all that's familiar, a daily battle for the basics of life, sometimes even homelessness. For the more economically privileged, city life brings the novelty of consumerism and acquisition, and all the secular "pleasures" that were once unobtainable in China.

For Seventh-day Adventists, this is the uncertain, rapidly shifting ground on which they must pursue their calling to be Christ's witnesses.

CLOSING DOORS

Beginning in 1950, the door to traditional missionary work in China began to gradually close, and the Seventh-day Adventist Church soon faced an incredibly nuanced and challenging mission landscape.

Prior to this time, Adventist missionaries worked throughout China. Pioneer Abraham LaRue led the way in 1888, followed in 1902 by missionary J. N. Anderson, who organized the first Adventist congregation in China and ordained the first Chinese minister.

With communism, however, came a new era that was hostile to both foreign influences and religion, and thus antithetical to the work of the Adventist Church. Over the ensuing years, the government developed the Three-Self Patriotic Movement as an umbrella regulatory organization for Protestant faiths within China, designed to insulate faith from foreign influence and to nurture a more home-grown, self-sufficient form of Protestantism.

Today, there are an estimated 420,000 Seventh-day Adventists in China who practice their faith both within and outside the formal structures of the Three-Self Patriotic Movement. There is no formal structural bond between Chinese Adventists and the broader Adventist world church—the bond that does exist between them is one of faith, mission, and familial love.

How, then, given the dramatic social and economic transformations taking place in China, and the complex political situation, can Chinese Adventists engage in urban mission? How can they stay faithful to Christ's command to take His message of compassion and salvation into the cities?

It would be fair to assume that with all these complexities to negotiate, urban ministry in China must follow an equally complex paradigm.

And yet, that assumption would be incorrect.

"IT'S RELATIONAL"

Elder Robert (Bob) Folkenberg, Jr. is president of the Seventh-day Adventist Church's Chinese Union Mission, based in Hong Kong. Both Bob and his wife, Audrey, speak Chinese and, having lived in China, Taiwan, and Hong Kong for many years, they're familiar with the culture. They also have a passion for establishing Adventist work within often neglected urban areas. In the three years since Bob began work at the Chinese Union Mission, the number of Global Mission pioneer teams of Chinese nationals working in China has doubled to some 220, with most of these operating within urban settings.

"China has big cities, very big cities, and massive cities," says Bob. He jokes that some of the apartment complexes in China are larger than entire cities in other places.

In spite of, or perhaps because of, the complicated environment in which pioneers operate, their *modus operandi* is simplicity itself.

"All city evangelism in China is relational evangelism," says Bob. "It's Christ's method alone: mingling with people, showing sympathy, ministering to their needs, winning their confidence, and then bidding them to 'follow Him.' "

Some Adventists in the West assume that all evangelistic activity is forbidden to Adventists in China, but the reality is far more textured—and freer—than many believe. Certainly, the Chinese government does not look with favor on foreign influences on religious activity. Yet the window of opportunity for witness in China is now wider than it has been for many years.

For instance, Adventists who worship within the framework of the Three-Self Movement can now hold some types of outreach meetings, although this, in itself, hasn't led to a huge increase in the number of evangelistic meetings. Earlier decades of tighter restrictions on religious practice mean that Adventists in China are neither familiar nor comfortable with the public evangelism model. As a starting point, Adventists are being encouraged to start opening their churches for an evening meeting during the week rather than focusing only on the two Sabbath meetings they usually hold.

Some forms of outreach remain difficult, though, for many different reasons. Pioneers who aren't functioning within the Three-Self Movement cannot simply go to their unentered territory and start preaching. Residency laws don't allow this type of movement. Also, there are restrictions on the amount of religious material that can be publicly distributed, although person-to-person distribution is now generally fine.

Adventist workers may not be able to do all those things we typically think of when it comes to evangelism, says Bob. But he points out that some of the challenges of urban outreach in China are not unique—secularism, materialism and humanism are as rampant as in the cities of the West.

"The Chinese economy is growing so fast that the money, power, and influence that comes with economic success is the number-one passion for most Chinese people," explains Bob. There's an additional challenge, also, that stems from the communist mindset, which "minimizes the importance of religion and, at times, makes faith incompatible with receiving job promotions in many companies and markets." He points out that China lacks the West's widespread cultural and historical associations with Christianity. Without this Christian heritage to draw on, pioneers face a blank slate when it comes to sharing and explaining their faith.

"By far the most successful method of reaching people in China is through meeting their needs," says Bob. He explains that the church in China uses personal work as their main church growth tool. "Most of our centers of influence are based on meeting people's health needs," he says. "They sell health foods, do health counseling and training. Many of our pioneers are using this method as well."

The stories that Bob and Audrey hear back from those who live, work, and witness in many urban centers throughout China demonstrate the tremendous power of compassionate, prayer-led "relational evangelism."

SCENE 1—A CITY IN SOUTHERN CHINA

In one of China's largest cities, among the millions who eke out an existence, live Mr. and Mrs. Li.[2] They came to the city a number of years earlier to find work but ended up finding much more than they bargained for. Somehow Mr. and Mrs. Li connected with Adventist believers in the city and, through them, found a profound sense of joy and hope in Christ. They decided to dedicate themselves to His work and began looking for a way to make connections within their community.

They decided to open a homeless shelter, and they named it the House of Love. Mr. and Mrs. Li regularly go out of an evening searching for homeless people, talking with them, sharing food, getting to know the "regulars" and, eventually, inviting them to come and stay.

Once there, homeless men and women not only receive a bed and something to eat, but many unexpected "extras"—including exercise classes, Bible stories, learning to sing hymns, and a sense of love and acceptance.

One man whose life was forever changed by the House of Love later wrote about his experience. He had grown up in a poor rural province and, when still young, had suffered an additional misfortune—a stroke that paralyzed his right side. Although he eventually regained his mobility, he was left with some permanent disability. Unable to carve out a life for himself in his home village, he followed the streams of young people heading toward the city.

"Suddenly, I was alone," he wrote. "Because of my physical disabilities, I could not find a job and began to wander the streets. I watched scavengers and learned how to become a scavenger myself, so that I could earn a little bit of money to live. And 'survival' was as good as it got."

One evening as the young man settled down to sleep in a bus shelter, Mrs. Li came by, spoke to him, and gave him some food. Each Saturday she returned, often with her husband, and the young man came to trust them. When they offered him a place to live, the young man said, "Yes."

"I was led by a kind gentleman onto a subway and was heading 'home,' " he wrote later about his experience. "My heart was uneasy, but when the door opened and happy faces greeted me, and I heard voices say, 'Welcome to The House of

---

2 The names and places associated with all the stories in this chapter have been changed.

Love,' those uneasy feelings completely vanished. I cannot describe the joy and warmth I felt. Tears began to fill my eyes, and soon they spilled over and ran down my cheeks."

Over the following days, the young man received a Bible and began to learn about the faith of his hosts.

"I know now that they could do this only because they believed in God, were filled with His love, and wanted to share . . . His grace with me, just as they themselves had received His grace. That's why they were willing to preach the Gospel to every person in need. That's why they invited me to their House of Love."

"My life has been changed," he adds. "I have been touched and want to be like them. I, too, believe in God and His Son."

SCENE 2—A CITY IN EASTERN CHINA

When Maeli and Shouling, two young Adventist pioneers, traveled to their assigned territory to start a new group of believers, they first went door to door, visiting every family in the neighborhood. Day after day, as they knocked on doors, the two young women discovered a startling pattern—at many of the houses they visited they met teenage girls living alone.

These young girls were some of the millions of children and young people in China sometimes called the Left-Behind Children—victims of the rapid urbanization that's changing the face of Chinese society. As parents are forced to leave rural areas or go to other urban areas in search of work, these children are left to care for themselves, or they're left with a nominal caregiver—often an elderly person who's physically or financially unable to provide the necessary care.

Maeli and Shouling began to get to know some of these young girls and the hardships they endured. They'd been left to fend for themselves, and, not surprisingly, they were often vulnerable to physical exploitation.

Together, Maeli and Shouling shaped their ministry around providing practical care for these left-behind girls. They visited them regularly, helped them wash clothes, and cooked for them. They invited the girls to their own home, where they played hymns and told Bible stories. Before long, Maeli and Shouling began to hold regular prayer times each afternoon after the girls had finished their homework. And it wasn't long before many of the girls were attending church and worshipping God each Sabbath morning.

Whenever any of the girls' parents returned to visit, Maeli and Shouling made contact with them. These young Adventists talked to the parents about how their daughter had been faring and alerted them to any difficulties.

Through their efforts, Maeli and Shouling developed a strong rapport not only with the young girls they cared for but also with their parents. The two Adventist workers helped lift some of the load of worry the parents carried with them as they worked in cities far away.

For Maeli and Shouling, there has been tremendous joy in sharing Christ with these left-behind girls and their families. So far, their practical ministry has led to 10 baptisms, and they give an average of 15 Bible studies every week.

SCENE 3—THE STREETS OF AN UNNAMED CHINESE CITY

The children wander almost unnoticed through main thoroughfares and narrow alleyways. They're on a mission, searching through bits and pieces that other people have discarded. They're looking for anything they can salvage and resell, anything that may earn them a little bit of money they can take back to their families who live in the rural villages surrounding the city.

"Why aren't these kids in school?" That was the question asked by Mr. and Mrs. J, an Adventist couple who had recently moved to the city with the goal of sharing Jesus in this unentered area.

Each day, Mr. and Mrs. J observed the children as they continued their never-ending search through the trash piles of the city.

Poverty in China is a complicated issue. Income disparity between city-dwellers and their rural counterparts is not new, but the size of this gap has grown even more dramatic in recent years as the government has introduced economic reforms. By Chinese measures, poverty is defined as those living on less than 2,300 yuan a year, or a little over $1 a day—a level of bare subsistence currently endured by some 200 million Chinese.[3]

For Mr. and Mrs. J, however, these children were more than mere statistics. As they thought about these boys and girls picking through the city rubbish, their compassion grew. Not only were the children scraping for the basics of life, but they were missing out on the benefits of an education, the only means by which the spiral of poverty from one generation to the next could be broken.

Slowly, Mr. and Mrs. J connected with the children and their families, gaining their trust and, finally, offering to provide free tutoring for the children.

Today, Mr. and Mrs. J teach almost 100 children reading, writing, arithmetic—and Jesus' love for children. Often Mr. and Mrs. J have the chance to share their message of healing and hope with the children's parents, and several have already been baptized and joined the worldwide body of Adventist believers.

---

3   Didi Kirsten Tatlow, "Despite Poverty Efforts, China Still Faces Income Gap," *New York Times,* October 17, 2014.

PINPOINTS OF LIGHT
WITHIN THE CITIES OF CHINA

Lessons from the front lines of urban mission

China's political and social setting may be unique, but when it comes to ministry and outreach, there are key similarities with urban outreach in the West. Materialism, the multi-faceted impact of poverty, the lack of a Christian heritage on which to "hang" witnessing efforts—these are all shared challenges for urban missionaries everywhere.

For Global Mission pioneers in Chinese cities, the key is relational outreach, an approach that centers on building trust through long-term relationships that address real needs.

Or, to put it more simply, in Ellen White's words that Pastor Folkenberg quotes, "It's Christ's method alone."

You can find out more information about the work of the Seventh-day Adventist Church's Chinese Union Mission at www.chumadventist.org/eng/.

CHAPTER 9

WORTHY OF THEIR LOVE AND CONFIDENCE

*In the center of one of the world's largest cities,
Adventists are creating a haven of hope.*

BETTINA KRAUSE[1]

*P*ROSTITUTES, CRIMINALS, THE HOMELESS—*these are not just charity cases for workers at one Seventh-day Adventist Center of Influence. Each person who crosses the threshold of the Hope Center in Mexico City is treated as a beloved child of God.*

HISTORICAL DOWNTOWN DISTRICT, MEXICO CITY

It's a large, plain room with a cement floor and whitewashed walls, illuminated by the severe glow of fluorescent lights. The room is filled with a series of plastic trestle tables set close together, each surrounded by a mismatched collection of metal and plastic chairs.

Every seat is taken. There are old men, teenagers, middle-aged women, and children. One elderly man leans his elbows on the table and rests his head on his hands. He has short-cropped hair and is wearing a gray sweatshirt that has seen better days. His face is etched with deep lines. At a nearby table sits a family: a mother and father with three young children. The youngest boy—no more that two years of age—sits on his mother's lap. She looks tired.

A pastor calls out from the front of the room and asks everyone to stand to give thanks to God for the food that's about to be served. As the pastor prays, most people in the crowded room stand with bowed heads, although one young man with unshaven face and dirty shirt stares straight ahead, face expressionless. At the end of the prayer, he murmurs, "Amen."

There's a vinyl banner strung up on one wall of the room with the name of this

---

1 Special thanks to Samuel Telemaque, director of the Office of Adventist Mission for the Inter-American Division, and Libna Stevens, assistant director, communication department of the Inter-American Division, for their assistance with this chapter.

Center of Influence spelled out in large letters. It's the Hope Center, or *Centro de Esperanza*. And many of the people gathered here tonight for one of the regular hot meals served by Seventh-day Adventists volunteers are in desperate need of hope.

AN URBAN LEVIATHAN

"I walk and do not move forward.
I am surrounded by city. I lack air . . ."[2]

This is how renowned Mexican poet Octavio Paz described the sensory overload that is Mexico City—the largest urban center in the Western hemisphere. It's crowded, chaotic, and claustrophobic. Or as another writer puts it, more prosaically, "Life in Mexico City is a contact sport."[3] It's a city of extremes—of wealth and poverty, religiosity and secularism, youthful optimism and human wretchedness.

It's difficult to adequately describe the immensity of this city, which has become synonymous the world over with scarcely restrained urban growth. In the words of one visitor, its sheer size "hits you in the face before your plane has even landed." The greater metropolitan area of some 9,600 square kilometers (3,700 square miles) embraces almost 23 million residents—roughly equivalent to Australia's total population, or to the populations of Portugal and Belgium combined.

Tourists to Mexico City tend to make a beeline for its historic center, with its eclectic collection of grand architecture—a mix of everything from baroque to neoclassical to Art Deco—spanning six centuries of urban development. At the heart of this historic center, tourists and locals walk through the massive square known as Zocalo, the largest city plaza in Latin America, which is edged by some of the nation's most important public buildings.

Another building not too far away, also located in the historic downtown, is not included in any tourist guide. Behind the unremarkable façade of the *Centro de Esperanza*, faithful Seventh-day Adventists are putting Christ's method of ministry into practice and demonstrating in practical ways Christ's unwavering love for this city and its residents.

LOCATION, LOCATION, LOCATION

Like real estate, the first consideration of a Center of Influence is location, and by that criterion, the *Centro de Esperanza* is perfectly positioned. This small Adventist Center of Influence lies at the crossroads of a vast human tragedy—part of which is visible but much of which is hidden.

To the east is the well-known La Merced Market, a centuries-old marketplace still in

---

2 Octavio Paz, "Immemorial Landscape," in *A Draft of Shadows and Other Poems* (New York: New Directions Publishing, 1979), 61.

3 Daniel Hernandez, *Down and Delirious in Mexico City* (New York: Scribner, 2011), 2.

use today. It's a chaotic world unto itself, filled with stalls displaying fresh produce and goods of all descriptions, resounding with the shouts of vendors, and bursting with the press of customers and tourists.

Visitors to the market will also see hundreds of children and youth. Some are juggling, others peddle snacks, some perform acrobatics or even put on fire-breathing shows—all in the hope that they can convince passers-by to toss them a peso or two.

EXTENDING MORE THAN CHARITY

Lessons from the front lines of urban mission

- **Location and mission must be intertwined.** The needs of those who live immediately around the Center of Influence should determine the services that are offered. Don't neglect demographic research.
- **Attitude matters.** When we serve others, we're not condescending or "doing them a favor." No matter what their background or current circumstances, we all share a common Father.
- **Extend friendship.** It is not just charity; it is key to winning trust.
- **Build a strong and wide base of volunteers.** By involving Adventist members from nearby churches, you're sharing a vision for urban mission and may help to seed new Centers of Influence.

These are some of Mexico City's estimated 30,000 street children. They live—or rather, survive—in loosely formed groups of homeless children. What shelter they have is sometimes as rudimentary as a few dirty sheets strung together to screen themselves from passing traffic. They have little or no education, few options for earning money, and no prospects for anything better. An estimated 90 percent of these young street children are addicted to industrial solvents or other drugs. For them, it's a temporary escape from a daily cycle of hopelessness.

To the west of the *Centro de Esperanza* lies the district of Tepito, notorious for centuries as a center of criminal activity. It's called locally Barrio Bravo or "fierce neighborhood." Most crimes today revolve around petty theft, counterfeiting, and product piracy rather than the robberies that gave the area its reputation, but violence in the area still often flares. For residents of Tepito, poverty and crime are ever-present.

Encircling *Centro de Esperanza* is a series of red light districts, where prostitution is rampant. Many of those being abused are just children. It's a tragedy of immense scope. Accompanying the exploitation of these women and children is a catalog of social ills—various diseases, alcohol and drug addiction, and more crime.

The neighborhoods around *Centro de Esperanza* are also filled with the homeless. Some are second- or even third-generation homeless who only know life on the streets of the city. Others are Mexicans from rural areas who are drawn to Mexico City in search of new opportunities yet find themselves without work or a place to live.

The Gospel of Matthew describes Jesus going through all the cities and villages, teaching in synagogues, proclaiming the gospel of the kingdom, and healing every kind of disease and every kind of sickness (Matt. 9:35). The next verse records that as Jesus saw the crowds of people, "he had compassion on them, because they were harassed and helpless, like sheep without a shepherd." This is the compassion that Adventists in Mexico City are striving to bring to the harassed and helpless men, women, and children who walk the streets of the historical downtown district.

"OUR SPECIAL FRIENDS"

The *Centro de Esperanza* project, launched in 2014, is the first of what local Adventist leaders hope will be many Centers of Influence scattered throughout Mexico City. It has its roots in a project of the Central Seventh-day Adventist Church, which in 2010 planted a new church in the downtown historical district. Led by church members Ignacio Rosas and Santos Gomez, the new congregation rented a facility and set it up with a dual purpose—it would serve as both a church and a place where indigent men, women, and children could find physical and spiritual help.

Their outreach and restoration project grew, and of the many people who came to the church for help of various kinds, some ultimately found something far more valuable: their Savior. A number of these once-homeless men and women are now active in local Adventist churches, and one is even leading out in a new church plant in another part of Mexico City.

By 2013, though, local Adventist leaders felt that even more could, and should, be done to bring Christ's love to the forgotten people of the streets of Mexico City.

The church's Metropolitan Conference, supported by the Central Mexican Union and the Inter-American Division, purchased the property on Ferrocarril de Cintura Street and appointed a full-time manager, Pastor Raul Moscoso. The overall coordination of the center was entrusted to Pastor Jaivez Munoz and Pastor Tomas Torres of the Central Mexico Union.

Their first task? To survey the territory surrounding the center and identify major needs. After study and prayer, the leadership team chose to focus on four groups found within a short radius of the center—prostitutes, homeless children, criminals, and indigent adults.

For these people, *Centro de Esperanza* provides services that help restore a sense of dignity and comfort. The center has built two full bathrooms for the use of the homeless, where they can shower and care for personal hygiene. The center also provides haircuts and runs health workshops aimed at the specific challenges of these impoverished men and women.

The center distributes donated clothes and warm blankets, and twice a week, on Tuesdays and Sundays, local churches and charities help the center provide a full hot meal for the homeless of the district.

For prostitutes, the *Centro de Esperanza's* long-term goal is to provide classes to train them in a trade that generates income and allows them to break free of a lifestyle that seems as inescapable as it is hopeless.

Workers at the center soon realized that many of those involved in crime in the area are addicted to various substances—anything from illegal narcotics to solvents to alcohol. Therefore, leaving behind a life of crime means first tackling a daunting task—breaking addictions. This is where *Centro de Esperanza* is focusing, offering emotional and spiritual support, health programs, and job listings for those who want to find a way out of their current lifestyle.

Beyond physical help, the center also holds regular spiritual meetings, such as the Ten-Minute Devotions, which attract many who come to hear more about the Creator who loves them. The facility also still operates as a church, and members meet each Sabbath in a hall on the property. But the signage and set-up of the facility are all aimed at drawing people in and making them feel at home. Pastor Javier Munoz, one of the coordinators of the project, explains that people who come to the center see it not primarily as a church but as a place where they receive kindness and care. And these are two functions he sees as entirely complementary.

Perhaps one of the most profound gifts the center gives those it serves, however, is the gift of acceptance. To the staff and volunteers of *Centro de Esperanza*, the people who walk through the front door seeking help aren't clients, customers, or even visitors. Each team member calls them, affectionately, "our special friends."

LESSONS FROM THE PAST

There's a poetic symmetry to the fact that Seventh-day Adventists in Mexico City are now focusing on Centers of Influence as a way of sharing Christ in the city. More than a hundred years ago, three Adventist missionaries to Mexico founded a small Center of Influence—an English language school—and thus established the first permanent Adventist work in Mexico City.

George W. Caviness was an educator and linguist who had been president of Battle Creek College. He traveled to Mexico in 1896 as part of a group of interdenominational scholars who were revising the Spanish translation of the Bible. Later, Caviness moved on to the Adventist Church's Guadalajara Clinic, where he helped develop the fledgling publishing ministry.

For Caviness, though, Mexico's largest urban area beckoned, and he, along with two assistants, moved to Mexico City in 1899 and opened an English language school. From this small beginning, the Adventist Church gained a foothold in this city of then around 500,000 people. In 1903, Caviness organized the Mexican Conference.

Caviness and his fellow missionaries regularly wrote back to the "home field" with reports that were sometimes published in the *Review and Herald* journal, describing the challenge of this mission territory.

So many statements by these early Adventist workers in Mexico seem to echo today's discussions about urban mission. As you read their letters to the church members back home, it's clear that, without explicitly naming it, they had adopted Christ's method of reaching people—mingling with people, caring for their needs, showing sympathy, gaining confidence, and then bidding people to follow their Savior.

"It is an impossibility to reach people [here] by the ordinary methods in vogue in our native land [America]," declared one missionary to Mexico in 1900. He suggests that Adventist Church members could move to Mexico and be "living epistles" and "by words of kindness and deeds of love, the true Christian life would be illustrated before the people."[4]

He advocated "close contact with the afflicted and the destitute, leading them, as we may be able, to the Lamb of God." Adventists should "by loving service prove that we are worthy of love and confidence."[5]

Today, the *Centro de Esperanza* follows in the steps of these pioneers and is offering "loving service" and winning confidence in the heart of Mexico City.

WINNING TRUST

As the reach of *Centro de Esperanza* grows, it is helping transform more than the lives of those it serves. Seventh-day Adventists from surrounding churches who volunteer here are catching a fresh vision for ministry and service, and they're sharing their discoveries with their fellow church members.

"This ministry differs a lot to what has been done in the past to reach out to people," say Pastor Javier Munoz, co-coordinator of *Centro de Esperanza*. "The church usually focuses on preaching the gospel through evangelistic campaigns only. Now there are many church members involved who have decided to use their God-given gifts to serve others and share God's love."

Javier says the ministry "allows us to come close to people, meet their needs, and once we win their trust, show them the way to salvation."

He says church members have changed their attitude about ways to relate to the community. They're volunteering to serve in the center, and the presence of *Centro de Esperanza* has ignited a desire to open other Centers of Influence in the city—perhaps focused on reaching people within different socioeconomic groups.

LOVE IN ACTION

At the *Centro de Esperanza*, the pastor has finished thanking God for the food, and dinner is now being served. There's controlled chaos in the small kitchen area at one end of the hall as three Adventist women ladle bean and vegetable soup into bowls, loading up the trays for volunteers who are waiting to serve their "special friends." Dessert has already been prepared—one bench of the kitchen is covered by scores of

---

4 A. Allen John, "Mexico," *Advent Review and Sabbath Herald,* May 8, 1900, 12.

5 Ibid.

plastic cups filled to the brim with cut fruit.

The elderly man in the old gray sweatshirt reaches up to take a large, steaming bowl of soup from a young woman carrying a serving tray. She moves to the table with the young family and places bowls in front of the mother and father, then in front of two of the children. One of the little boys looks up and smiles.

CHAPTER 10

EVERYONE EATS LUNCH

*A once impenetrable barrier between
a church and its community is broken down.*

KWON JOHNGHAENG

*T*HE CHURCH STOOD ON EXPENSIVE PROPERTY *in the cultural and economic center of Seoul, home to some 10 million people. The challenge? A profound disconnection between the church and its community. Could a simple, everyday need help bridge the gap?*

JONGNO, SEOUL, SOUTH KOREA

For many years, the Seoul Central Seventh-day Adventist Church was an island amid a sea of office buildings, shops, and historic landmarks. This large, well-built structure seemed to stand apart from its high-energy neighborhood. It exuded a sense of stillness. Most weeks, the church doors opened just three times: on Sabbaths for worship services, on Tuesdays for prayer meeting, and on Friday evenings for vespers. For the rest of the week, the church stood quiet and unused.

Jongno, the area where Central church is located, is one of the oldest and most celebrated areas of Seoul. In fact, the name of this district has become synonymous in the Korean language with "town square," a result of Jongno's 600-year history as the cultural, economic, religious, and political epicenter of the city. Jongno is home to some of the country's most iconic buildings. There's the chief temple of the Jogye Order of Korean Buddhism, along with other shrines, and no fewer than five palaces from past dynasties of Korean rulers.

Today, towering corporate headquarters and busy shopping areas add a 21st-century feel to this ancient town center. Traffic noise dominates the senses, and the sidewalks are filled with office workers, shoppers, and tourists.

What seems like an enviable location, however, has significant drawbacks for a church. Few of the almost 600 people who regularly attend Central church actually live in Jongno; most have to travel from nearby residential districts. In fact, there is very little "community" to speak of in the area immediately surrounding the church.

For a mission-minded church, this location presented a formidable challenge. How could members of a "commuter congregation" be engaged in community outreach? And, even more perplexing, how could they be "salt and light" for Jesus within a transient community of office workers that arrived on weekday mornings and departed again in the evening?

This was a situation that had developed gradually, year by year. For more than a century, this church had occupied an important place in the history of the Seventh-day Adventist Church in Seoul, tracing its roots back to one of the first companies of believers established in the city. Through the decades, it had always been an active and engaged congregation, and its central location in a well-known district proved an advantage.

Then, as the demographic makeup of the neighborhood around it began to change—as more offices were built, and more residents left—Central church tried to adapt. It ran evangelistic events, it tried literature distribution, it offered health and wellness programs. Still, the disconnect between community and church continued to grow.

By 2002, many church members were discouraged. Sabbath attendance was still high, yet the church building itself seemed underutilized, and its impact in the community was minimal. The congregation embarked on a period of prayer, asking God to use them and their church, with all its apparent drawbacks, to truly make a difference in their community.

The breakthrough finally came with a simple realization: everyone eats lunch.

A FRESH IDEA

Urban mission in Seoul comes with the usual challenges of city outreach anywhere around the world: people with too much to do and too little time to explore spiritual concerns; the distractions of a strong consumer culture; the skepticism that many Gen Xers and Millennials have toward institutional religion. And then for Adventists in Korea, there's an added layer of difficulty when it comes to city ministry: the deep-seated wariness many feel toward the Adventist faith.

Korea is a tolerant, multi-religious society that embraces traditional religions, including shamanism, Buddhism, and Confucianism. And over the past century, Christianity—especially evangelical Christianity—has also become a significant force. Korea is the most "Christianized" Asian nation, with Christians making up about a quarter of the population. But among the Christian denominations, the Adventist Church is numerically small and tends to be isolated by others' preconceptions and biases.

So when, in 2002, the then-senior pastor of Central church suggested a lunchtime natural foods restaurant for nearby office workers, not everyone in the congregation was immediately convinced it would work. The church had tried something similar before but found it wasn't easy to attract people onto the church premises.

A NICHE MINISTRY WITH A HUGE IMPACT

Lessons from the front lines of urban mission

- **Quality counts.** When it comes to providing a service to urbanites, remember they usually have other options, and thus top-notch quality is essential. In the early years of Seoul Central church's restaurant ministry, the regular chef left and was replaced by a less-skilled cook. As the food quality declined, so did the daily number of guests. Quickly, the church found another cook and reversed the slide in numbers. But it was a reminder that ministries in an urban setting must take marketplace forces into account. For a restaurant ministry, that means meeting expectations in regard to quality and service. For Central church, located in the midst of many other cafés and restaurants, this is especially important to remember.

- **Find a niche.** Along with quality, another key to success is finding and meeting a niche need. For Central church, this meant identifying the desire of office workers for fresh, inexpensive, and healthy lunches, but every community has unique unmet needs, says Pastor Park SangKil. "I believe we need to accurately assess the needs of the community and provide distinguished, superior solutions. People won't step into church to eat unless we provide something no one else can."

- **Be creative.** Setting up a ministry will be difficult. There will be hurdles, not least of which will be identifying a community need and matching it with the resources you have within your church. Once a ministry is actively meeting a real need, though, its success will be largely self-perpetuating.

- **Don't give up.** It may take a long time and a number of failed experiments before you finally hit upon the unique need that your church is equipped to meet. But with prayer and trust in God's leading, be confident that He will ultimately take your efforts and use them to build His kingdom in your community.

But Pastor Kim Daesung persisted. "As I was thinking about how to make contact with the people who work nearby, I thought that it could be very practical if we operated a restaurant because most of the people would want to eat lunch," he later wrote about his involvement with the project. "I was thinking that if we provide very fresh food, friendly food—like a family—the people will like it."

He reminded his members about Ellen White's counsel to start Centers of Influence, such as restaurants, in urban areas. And when he gained the support of his congregation, they set to work.

Central church already had the space—a large fellowship hall with many tables and chairs, and a modern, well-equipped kitchen. But there was one seemingly insurmountable problem: under Korean law, it was difficult for a nonprofit church organization to own and operate a restaurant.

Central church, however, came up with a creative solution. They decided that instead of opening a traditional restaurant, they would set up a "health association."

Essentially, it was a lunch club—members would pay a monthly fee that would entitle them to eat their weekday lunches at the church.

For the next three months, the pastor and church members visited surrounding offices, meeting with hundreds of workers one by one, and presenting this unusual proposal. The membership fee was set at the equivalent of about US$100 per month, and, in exchange, the office worker was promised fresh, tasty, and healthy vegetarian lunches Monday through Friday.

There was immediate interest, and even more so when the church distributed some 600 meal tickets for a free lunch during the restaurant's opening week.

The hard work paid off. On opening day, a line of almost 500 guests snaked around the corner of the building—some 200 more than had been expected. As the workers enjoyed their free meal, the pastor encouraged them to sign up for a membership so they could eat there every day. The response was overwhelming, and with that, the Seoul Central church Center of Influence was launched.

ISOLATED NO MORE

From the outset, Central church committed itself to providing only the highest quality food and service, and this insistence on excellence has paid off. Six paid staff members are employed, assisted by a regular rotation of church member volunteers who help in the kitchen or in the dining area. Together, they turn out a daily vegetarian feast. Colorful platters of salads, breads, and warm foods are laid out for guests, and inviting smells waft outside to those lining up for a table.

More than 200 people visit the church every day for lunch. The attractive space is filled with people eating, talking, and laughing together. The atmosphere is relaxed and comfortable. Over the years, the clientele has diversified and now includes artists, Buddhist monks from a nearby temple, business executives, and wealthy middle-aged women, as well as office and government workers.

The quality of the food soon led to catering requests, and the restaurant is often rented out for alumni meetings and even pastors' meetings of other Christian denominations.

Pastor Park SangKil, senior pastor of Seoul Central church, makes a point of visiting the restaurant each lunch time, greeting people, meeting newcomers, and chatting with regulars. It's an unparalleled opportunity to mix with people who would otherwise never set foot in an Adventist church, he says.

Regular customers have developed a fierce loyalty to the restaurant. "Some days can get really busy for our volunteers, and so some of our regulars even help out with serving!" says Park SangKil. "The atmosphere of the restaurant is so friendly and welcoming that we hardly ever get any complaints if the food is served late. Some visitors tell us they'd rather skip lunch if they can't get to the restaurant; they say they'd rather go hungry than eat an unhealthy meal."

For Park SangKil, the restaurant represents a "golden opportunity" to share the Adventist faith and culture with the community—especially with those of a socio-economic background whom the church has previously found almost impossible to reach. "The church used to be open only a few times a week," he adds. "Now the church is open all week and is full of people who come to have needs fulfilled."

Many have been baptized as a direct result of this ministry, and others have expressed interest in Bible studies. Yet the real impact of this Center of Influence can't be measured solely in terms of baptisms. For Pastor Park and members of the Central church, one of the most significant outcomes of the restaurant has been a sea change in community attitudes toward the Seventh-day Adventist Church. Old prejudices have been swept away and replaced with friendship. Disinterest has been replaced by curiosity. Suspicion has been replaced by acceptance.

Through the years, the church has received a lot of feedback from regular visitors, many of whom once thought of Adventists as "odd people" and now consider them to be "warmhearted, kind people" who are committed to living by biblical principles.

Central church uses its restaurant to display Adventist literature and information about the health food products regularly used in the restaurant. The church's head deaconess, Mrs. Cho ByungSoon, holds monthly cooking demonstrations, and these have proved very popular. Those who attend the cooking classes are later invited to participate in a health evangelism program, which has led to people requesting Bible studies and later joining the church.

"There are tremendous opportunities to plant the Advent message in the hearts of our visitors," says Pastor Park. "And, just as importantly, our church members have also learned the joy of serving the community."

"INDESCRIBABLE JOY"

The success of the lunch restaurant has helped create spin-off ministry opportunities. First and foremost, it has provided funding for a special Sabbath ministry to elderly people who live in nearby districts. Each Sabbath morning, some 300 seniors attend a special worship service just for them at Central church and stay afterward for a fully catered free lunch. Over the years, church members have developed strong bonds with many of these elderly men and women, and some 40 of them have joined the church.

The church also gives a significant portion of income from the restaurant to the local government to help care for the district's orphan children—a gesture that fosters considerable goodwill for the church in the community. Money from the restaurant also helps a yearly youth mission trip to Nepal. The young people raise money for their own travel expenses, but funds from the lunch ministry pays for church construction.

Park SangKil has seen many of his church members grow spiritually as they've served in the restaurant ministry and become more confident in sharing their faith. "They're proud that their ministry contributes to the physical health of the community and serves as a bridge to sharing the gospel," he says.

Dr. Suh SoonSuk, an elder at the church, serves as a volunteer manager at the restaurant. For the past two years, his smiling presence has been a fixture at the restaurant as he's served at the tables and interacted with guests. "I'd like to see more churches open cafeterias to the public as Centers of Influence and to share the love of Christ with people," he says. "These days, it's very difficult to visit door to door in the big cities. But here they come to us and we meet them in our arena."

For Park SangKil, who continues to shake hands and chat with guests each day, it's difficult for him to describe the joy he feels at the sight of his church, which once stood empty and unused during the week, now filled to capacity with people from all walks of life.

And when he baptizes individuals who have come to know their Savior as a result of the church's restaurant ministry? "Words cannot express how I feel," he says. "There's nothing happier or more worthwhile than seeing someone accept Jesus Christ."

"FOLLOW ME"

"THE SAVIOR MINGLED WITH MEN AS ONE WHO DESIRED THEIR GOOD. HE SHOWED HIS SYMPATHY FOR THEM, MINISTERED TO THEIR NEEDS, AND WON THEIR CONFIDENCE. AND THEN HE BADE THEM, *'FOLLOW ME.'*"

ELLEN G. WHITE

"AS WE COME CLOSE TO PEOPLE BY LISTENING, meeting needs, and building relationships, they will desire to know the One we are revealing through our love. Inviting people to follow Jesus can be as simple as an invitation to church, a small group, or Bible study. Many times the answer to why someone has not made the next step in their spiritual journey and made a commitment to Christ is simply this: they have not yet been invited. It's essential to take the time to invite. 'Would you like to come?' 'Would you like to study?' 'Would you like to pray together?' Our service is not finished until we make an invitation to join us in following Jesus."

Tara VinCross is lead pastor of the REACH Philadelphia Seventh-day Adventist Church in Pennsylvania, United States, and director of the REACH Columbia Union Urban Evangelism School.

CHAPTER 11

FAR BEYOND FOUR WALLS

*A prayer-led spiritual awakening
has far-reaching consequences in Brazil*

FABRÍCIO FRANCISCO DE FRAGA AND SILAS GOMES DE OLIVEIRA NETO

*T*AKE A REGULAR SEVENTH-DAY ADVENTIST URBAN CHURCH.
*Add a deliberate focus on prayer and spiritual renewal. The result? A change in the
spiritual vision of an entire congregation, and a passion for mission that reaches
other cities, far from home.*

CURITIBA, BRAZIL

The recent history of Portão Seventh-day Adventist Church in Curitiba, Brazil, can be
divided into two distinct periods—before and after. In its "before" phase, Portão church
was a comfortable, prosperous church in an equally comfortable and prosperous city. With
1,200 members in the city's central area, Portão church was known for fine preaching,
excellent music, and well-planned events. But the focus was mainly on the needs of church
members, and little effort was made to connect with the broader community.

Today, in the "after" phase, Portão church is no longer merely four walls, a roof, and a
floor. It's a vibrant, living community of believers, sustained by prayer, and committed to
demonstrating Christ's wholistic ministry in unentered urban communities.

What marks the dividing line between before and after? The simple answer is prayer.

AN AFFLUENT MISSION FIELD

Viewed from above, the southern Brazilian city of Curitiba is a patchwork of tall
skyscrapers, historic buildings, and—tying everything together—vast swathes of green
parkland. The city sprawls out over a gently undulating plateau almost 300 meters
(1,000 feet) above sea level and is known around the world for its decades-long focus

on innovative urban planning. Although it is home to almost two million residents, the cosmopolitan city of Curitiba manages to blend both efficiency and aesthetic appeal, a combination that has earned it the title of "the world's most livable city."

The residents of Curitiba are known for being well educated, culturally sophisticated, and economically comfortable. It's little wonder, then, that Portão Adventist church, the second-largest Adventist church in the city, mirrored its community. Some in the church, however, were concerned about the fundamental attitude of their spiritual community.

PRE-DAWN PRAYERS

The turning point came with a season of prayer. In 2011, Pastor Silas Gomes de Oliveira Neto became pastor of the Portão church and, together with his leadership team, developed a pilot project called *Portão Global*. The project aimed to transform the way the church related to its community, so that its default focus was no longer inward but outward—toward the needs of non-members.

Rather than plunging directly into mission activity, church leaders announced a project called *Quarenta Madrugadas de Oração*—40 Dawns of Prayer. For 40 consecutive days, the doors of Portão church opened promptly at 5:30 A.M. for prayer. For these 40 days, many church members and friends got up early and made their way to the church to pray for the outpouring of the Holy Spirit. As they prayed and sought the Lord together, the Spirit responded. The outcome of this intense period of prayer was a spiritual "reset"—a revival—of the congregation. It marked a dramatic change in its vision for mission and service.

As a result of the 40 Dawns of Prayer, 40 people were baptized. Also, 80 church members committed to leave Portão church and go to a nearby suburb—*Água Verde*—to begin planting a new church there.

Água Verde, literally "Green Water," is a wealthy neighborhood with tree-lined streets, expensive shopping districts, and a reputation for being one of Curitiba's most elite areas. Over the weeks and months, the core group of church planters made friends, and their small group steadily grew. Five years later, the *Água Verde* Adventist Church has almost finished construction of a large, modern church building, with seating in the main sanctuary for 600 people.

This offspring of the Portão church is keeping alive the mother church's original vision for service and outreach. Alongside their new church, they plan to build a Center of Influence affiliated with the work of the Adventist Church's Novo Tempo television network. The facility, called Espaço Novo Tempo (Novo Tempo Venue), will offer spiritual, educational, and health support for the neighborhood.

THINKING BIG

In the wake of the 40 Dawns of Prayer and its launch of the *Água Verde* church plant, Portão church began to develop what it calls *Esperança Global*—Global Hope. This plan has ambitious goals: every year, Portão church seeks to reach into a com-

BEYOND THE BORDERS

Montevideo is the most secular city in the most secular country in South America—Uruguay. It has only a relative handful of Seventh-day Adventists and is one of 12 cities in Brazil, Uruguay, and Paraguay where *Esperança Global* ministry has shared the gifts and energy that God has given them.

Three buses filled with 135 people traveled from Curitiba to Montevideo to kick-start an urban mission project. They traveled nearly 1,000 miles, not as tourists but as disciples with a mission. In Montevideo they joined with and encouraged local church members to impact the community. They participated in one of the city's oldest street markets. Breaking into three groups, they handed out special cards, provided music, and gave free hugs. The cards were specially designed to connect spiritual things with one of Uruguay's great passions—football (soccer)—and featured Celeste, the Uruguayan national team.

Close by the street fair, another team of 20 people spent the morning helping a local public school. Collaborating with the local education department, they cleaned, pulled weeds, and painted walls.

Follow-up activities have included 15 members of the Portão church spending 20 days of their personal vacation time in Montevideo, working as volunteer Bible instructors. The Portão church provided free Spanish lessons for six months for those who wanted to participate in the Montevideo project.

munity with no Adventist presence, model Christ's method of ministry, and establish a new Adventist church.

Early on, leaders of Global Hope realized they'd need to build up a network of partners who could support the ministry. First, they found encouragement and backing for their efforts from the Seventh-day Adventist Church's Central Paraná Conference and South Brazil Union. Another faithful partner has been the Brazilian Red Cross, which provides equipment and medical specialists, as well as access to individuals who can often open doors for the ministry.

Within Portão church itself, two significant partners have been the *Instituto O Amor Chama*—the Love Calls Institute—and the *Chama Coral*—the Flame Choir ministry. *O Amor Chama* is a not-for-profit organization created by a group of friends who are members of the Portão church. It partners with the Adventist Development and Relief Agency (ADRA) and the Civil Defense of the State of Paraná, and is focused on social action. The group's projects are wide-ranging, creative, and practical. One recent event in the church hall saw hairdressers cut the hair of hundreds of volunteers, providing hair donations to make wigs for cancer patients. The *Chama Coral* is a 200-voice choir of the *Portão* church that works closely with *O Amor Chama*. The members of these two ministries, many of them young people, provide enthusiastic, hands-on support for the Global Hope projects.

SEVEN-STEP METHOD

Global Hope has developed an approach to working in urban communities based on principles drawn from Scripture and the counsel of Ellen White. It's consciously modeled on the way Jesus and His disciples moved among people, caring for their physical needs and drawing them into a relationship with their Creator.

After planting a church in *Água Verde,* the Portão church decided to focus next on Inácio Martins, a city some 130 miles from Curitiba. It was chosen in part because it was on a Global Mission list of cities in the State of Paraná with no Adventist presence. This first project outside the city of Curitiba set the pattern for subsequent projects and provides a good case study for the seven-step Global Hope method.

1. Mingling with people

After the city of Inácio Martins was chosen and all necessary arrangements were made with the city government, project leaders and local ADRA representatives began a campaign in Portão church to gather donations of nonperishable food and clothing. Then three buses carrying some 150 volunteers left Curitiba headed for Inácio Martins. They called this first stage "Impact Hope," during which the ministry teams from Portão church aimed to visit all the homes in the city, averaging some 2,000 visits each day.

The purpose of these visits was simply for the volunteers to talk with families in Inácio Martins, develop relationships, pray with them about their problems, and to understand what needs each family had. Before they left each home, the volunteers invited the families to attend a forthcoming *Expo Saúde*, or Health Fair.

2. Caring for needs

At the Health Fair, volunteers from Portão church offered a vast array of free services to the Inácio Martins community, including basic medical tests, dental and psychological consultations, legal services, haircuts and skin cleansing, group exercises, and spiritual counseling. For the children they provided a playground, popcorn and cotton candy, dramas and games, and the star attraction, Dr. Smile—a "medical clown."

As well as the various professionals who donated their time and skills at the Health Fair, other volunteers included personnel from the Red Cross and many Portão church members, including Pathfinders.

The day ended with a gospel concert provided by *Chama Coral*, followed by distribution of donated clothes and food. All of these activities took place in public schools or health centers around Inácio Martins.

The purpose of the Health Fair, say leaders of Global Hope, was to "relieve people's pain and enhance their self-esteem—even if it is for only one day." They add, "We wanted them to understand that we care about them, and we want their very best.

This helps us to create a relationship, and later on in the process the trust gained will help us in the process of asking them to follow Jesus."

3. Sharing Jesus

The third step involved Bible workers from Portão church, called *Mensageiros da Esperança*, or Messengers of Hope. They moved into Inácio Martins with their families to build on the public awareness created by the recent Health Fair. They also looked for a well-located auditorium in the community for a series of evangelistic meetings.

These Bible workers built friendships in the community and started spreading the word that long-term health and education projects, similar to those showcased at the Health Fair, would soon be established in the community. Organizers say this part of the process helped smooth the way for the coming evangelistic meetings.

4. Prayer

The fourth step took place back in the Portão church and was named *Pentecostes da Esperança*, or Pentecost of Hope. For 50 days the church held three daily worship services, spending one hour each at dawn, noon, and sunset in communion with God through prayer, hymns, and Bible study, seeking individual and collective spiritual revival. Throughout this period, the church served breakfast and lunch every day to all participants, and on some days, more than 300 people attended the noon service and stayed for lunch.

This intense period of prayer focused on a specific need—the Holy Spirit's guidance in the preparation for the upcoming evangelistic meeting.

5. Evangelism

The volunteers at Inácio Martins kept preparing for the upcoming citywide evangelistic program, which they called *Auditório da Esperança*, or Hall of Hope. Back at Portão church, the Pentecost of Hope program kept outreach front and center and helped church members feel a sense of participation and real connection with the project, even though it was taking place in another city.

In the city of Inácio Martins, some 400 people from the community attended the evangelistic programs each night. As interest grew, the team of Bible workers already in place within the community assisted Conference evangelist Pastor Julio Padilha in giving Bible studies. The result? At the end of the series, almost 90 people were baptized and a new church was established in the previously unentered town of Inácio Martins.

6. Building a church

A vital sixth step in the Global Hope method is to provide a place of worship for the new Adventist community. This can mean either building a new church or refurbishing an existing building.

7. Making disciples

The final step is called *Conservando a Esperança*, or Keeping the Hope. It is a long-term, ongoing effort to help new believers become true disciples and ministers, and it is crucial to the entire process. Here, new believers realize that baptism is just the start, that those who have been saved by Christ are now invited to participate in His work, learn from Him, and follow in His steps. This represents the end of one cycle and the beginning of a new one.

SHARING THE LOVE

Lessons from the front lines of urban mission

- **Base everything on prayer.** The foundation and orientation for all of Portão church's mission activities is prayer. Prayer started the mission movement, and prayer continues to sustain it.
- **Involve non-believers.** A key value of Portão church's outreach efforts is to involve community members as much as possible. A team of four professional hairdressers, who are not Adventists, have joined in every mission effort of the church.
- **Partner with government and community agencies.** Where possible, utilize the resources and experience of other agencies that are willing to work with you. Portão church has, for example, forged a valuable partnership with the Brazilian Red Cross.

To find out more about *Esperança Global* ministry, visit
www.esperancaglobal.com.br.

CHAPTER 12

THE CHURCH FOR THOSE WHO AREN'T HERE YET

With no permanent church building
of its own, this congregation is constructing
a "church for the unchurched."

NATHAN BROWN

*S*EVENTEEN YEARS AGO, A SEVENTH-DAY ADVENTIST CHURCH *in*
a struggling Australian community had dwindled to just three members. Today, in
the midst of this typically secular, urban neighborhood, a vibrant congregation of
more than 200 members is focused on demonstrating Christ's love in practical ways and is
training every church member for active ministry.

WYONG, NEW SOUTH WALES, AUSTRALIA

The smells of fried onions and vegeburgers hang in the warm afternoon air. People young and old are working on packing up the hall—stacking chairs, cleaning away the barbecues, emptying rubbish bins, sweeping floors. Most of those who worshipped in the morning are still there. The work seems unhurried and likely to be interrupted by conversations. The tasks seem less important than the people and, amid the quiet busyness, there are still a number of groups whose conversations continue.

It has been a long week for most of these people. Severe storms swept across their region, and the wind uprooted trees and downed power lines. Most people have spent some days without electricity, and they share stories of their week and of good-neighborliness. Some of the men are involved in the emergency response teams still out working in the surrounding communities, so they didn't make it to church this week. Amid it all, the calm of this Sabbath afternoon is something that can be felt among the groups having quiet conversations, and it's something that many seem unwilling to leave.

Appropriately, the Central Coast Community Church meets at the Oasis Youth Center in the business hub of Wyong, about 100 kilometers north of Sydney, Australia. The center itself has a story; it was built in response to the region recording the highest rates of youth suicide nationally for three years in a row. Wyong is one of those in-between communities, close enough to big-city social problems and suburban isolation but with too many small-town limitations and a struggling community identity.

It's a place in which the Adventist Church has always struggled. The story of Central Coast Community Church begins with the closure of the Wyong Seventh-day Adventist Church—and later the sale of the church building. The three remaining members voted it unanimously.

But they were also among the 30 people who signed up to the vision, mission, and values of a new church—and a new kind of church—that same day. One of them continues as an active member more than 17 years later.

Also among this group was Pastor Wayne Krause, now director of the South Pacific Division's Center for Church Planting. He had been the pastor of Mt. Colah, the most northerly Adventist church in Sydney, and his ministry had attracted a small number of families from the nearby Central Coast. Between them, they began talking about the challenges and opportunities for the church and community in their region.

"Our focus right from the start was to create a church that was for people who didn't normally go to church," Wayne says. He contacted the Conference administration, and the idea of a church plant began to grow. "We talked with the three members of Wyong and asked them what they wanted to do. They said they didn't care but that they wanted to reach the community, and we agreed that, by closing the church, we could get a new start. A lot of credit must go to those three faithful members and the sacrifice they were prepared to make."

As the transitions took place, Wayne and his wife, Tracey, and another family from the Mt. Colah church, moved to live on the Central Coast. Some 15 additional Mt. Colah members, some who lived on the Central Coast already, and others who were prepared to commute each Sabbath, joined this core group. They met together for almost a year before their first public worship service in February 1998, meeting in rented facilities. For the past 14 years, they have met in the Oasis Youth Center, which includes an auditorium and other meeting rooms, a gymnasium, and a skate park. The center was built by the local government and is operated during the week by the Salvation Army but rented by the church every weekend for Friday night and Sabbath.

Even the setting itself reminds the church members of what they set out to become. "We are very conscious that anyone might walk in to our worship service," explains head elder John Sanburg. "We expect it to happen every week, whether it is someone just curious about what is going on in here or some of the young people using the skate park. That changes how we welcome people, how we talk, what we do—everything we do is intentional."

And people have been baptized whose first contact with the church was simply walking in the door to see what was happening. Wes had been visiting family in

Ukraine when he first visited a Seventh-day Adventist church with a friend. Returning home, he went looking for an Adventist church, asking at the Salvation Army youth center if they could direct him to such a church. They told him to come back on Saturday morning. The first few weeks, he says, he sat as close as he could to the door—in case he needed to get out. Now he is part of the family.

Wayne explains that the early meetings were crucial to setting the DNA of the new church community. "We trained in how to share our faith with people, and learning that every member is a minister was a huge thing for us—and it still is," he says. "Everyone see themselves as a minister in whatever role they are fulfilling. Whether it's at home, whether it's at school, whether it's work, they see themselves as a minister. Their role is to make friends and to build authentic relationships."

After a number of public evangelism programs had been tried without success in the history of the Wyong church, the new group decided to invest their resources and time in other ways. "We decided that we would run no public programs for the first few years, and if anyone came to church, it would be because people brought them," Wayne recalls. "So the issue of making friends with unchurched people—friendships of integrity and authenticity—and people coming to church that way was important. We were not going to grow without that."

The way this was going to happen was by intentional involvement in the community. Wayne says he has never been part of a church with a higher proportion of people in some form of ministry, with church members involved in more than 100 different ministries in the church or the community. Not that the church necessarily runs all these ministries. As one member comments, "We don't drive many of these, but we support many things."

Many of the people are quick to share the stories of other church members. "You should talk to . . ." and mention someone's name. They are proud of how they see each other serving. There's the family who fosters boys short and long term; one of these boys brought his birth mother to his church, where she, too, is now a member; the young guy who has grown up in this church now heading off to a two-year commitment with a traveling music ministry; and the leader of the annual mission trips that many young people from the church make to a small town in rural New South Wales.

Grant is a young man who has chosen not to play football on Sabbath but has been signed to play semi-professionally because of the strength of character this stand demonstrates (as well as his ability on the field) and is using this as a way of connecting with his teammates and of bringing young people to the games to interact with better role models. He's also the church youth leader.

This kind of engagement with the community has brought opportunities the church would not have received in any other way. After the church ran a breakfast program at the local public school over a number of years, the school community insisted that if the school was to have a chaplain it had to be someone from Central

Coast Community Church. Recently, the local police have invited the church to run a program on weekend nights at the local railway station. Wayne says, "We have developed a reputation for being part of this community, working with the community, not just for them—and people respond to that."

The church leaders are quick to emphasize that this has not happened by accident. As pastor of a church without a permanent building, Wayne has taken this opportunity to set an example of simply being in the community. His office is a coffee shop at a nearby major shopping mall. He conducts Bible studies there, meets with people for pastoral visits and counseling, and church leadership meetings happen there during the week.

As opportunities have arisen in the past, Central Coast Community Church almost purchased a permanent facility on at least one occasion, but the deal did not go through. John says this is one of these ideas that comes and goes. They see the potential for a more comprehensive ministry with a permanent base but also the risks of becoming too settled and perhaps too focused on maintaining a building and all the issues that come with that. "We don't argue about what color our church carpet should be," John jokes, "because we simply don't have any carpet."

Like a number of the other long-time Adventist church members, John was looking for a more positive church environment after some difficult personal experiences. He found a home at Central Coast Community Church and was soon involved in leadership. Drawing on his professional background, he leads international mission trips to Cambodia, supported by the church, every second year. "We didn't want this focus to be all consuming, because it is a big task to get a group of us over there with planning and fundraising," he explains. "But we have seen the benefits of these trips in the impact it has on our people, as well as the projects we have been able to work on there."

Such a sense of mission also plays out at home. From the original group of 30, Central Coast Community Church has grown to as many as 300 people, although now has a Sabbath attendance near two hundred. Part of this "decline" has come with support of or contribution to six other church plants during their 17 years. These plants generally happen organically, when a group or family feel they would like to step out into this kind of mission, and they take different forms and styles. "It is often people who have been involved in leadership who want to take this next step," says Wayne, "so we have to have a culture of leadership development."

This begins in their weekly Kids' Church program. The 10-to-12 year-olds are encouraged to help run the program for the younger children, and when they move on to the teen and youth programs they are rostered to come back to assist with Kids' Church once a month. "We seem to keep our kids," John says, as he shows the Kid's Church set up and introduces its leaders. Wayne agrees. "Having been here 17 years, I am now baptizing young people who I dedicated as babies," he says. "This is the only church they have known, and it is part of who they are."

Kids' Church has been key to the church from the outset. On Sabbath mornings, the worship service begins at 10:00 A.M. with music and other worship, then splits into the sermon or Kids' Church for the under-12s, which then continues through the after-church Sabbath School discussion time. Kids' Church is interactive and energetic, focused on teaching basic Bible knowledge and values, as well as offering the first opportunities for ministry, service, and leadership.

Meanwhile, the main worship service is contemporary in style and based in the Bible, without assuming that worshippers have familiarity with what the Bible is or says. Page numbers are announced and come up on the screen to assist worshippers in finding their way through the Bibles that are made available to visitors. And one of the Sabbath School options is a group with the preacher of the day to talk about the sermon and ask questions they might have.

Lunch is served every week. It's a ministry in itself—dubbed "The Garden of Eating." Rather than a regular church potluck, it is organized on a roster basis with a rotating menu. The food is good and often attracts kids from the skate park and other passers-by. A relative newcomer to the church, Catherine leads this ministry. Recognizing its significance for the church community, she volunteered for the role when the previous leader moved away.

Because of the different format, the overlapping involvement with children in Kids' Church, and the offer of lunch, about 85 percent of church worshippers are actively involved in Sabbath School. A similar percentage of the church are also involved in small groups during the week. I am told that if I turn up at church for a few weeks, I will be invited and encouraged to join a group near where I live. These are considered a vital component of the life of the church. For some, this is their introduction to the community of faith, as well as what it means to be a follower of Jesus, and some of these groups have grown into house churches of their own.

Community is important, and John tells me how Facebook has become a valuable tool in keeping church members connected and connecting others. His wife, Melissa, takes photos of as many people as she can each week, and they are soon on Facebook. "If members are unable to be here one week, they can see who was here and what we did," John explains. "But we are also connecting with all our members' contacts. We've had people approach our members to ask about our church and about our faith purely because they have connected with our Facebook page."

So while there is a healthy reluctance to leave among the church members who are taking their time packing up on a calm Sabbath afternoon, Wayne is quick to point out that this is not primarily what their church is about. "We exist for those who aren't here yet," he says a number of times during our conversation. "As a young person, I wanted to be part of a church that reflected the biblical idea of community and that I would feel comfortable bringing my friends to—and I feel like I have been part of that for the past 17 years."

Wayne admits that working with unchurched people is often messy but that it also brings the greatest opportunities for transformation. "Seeing the power of the gospel to change people's lives has been the biggest thing for me," he says. "To watch the light go on in somebody's eyes when they actually realize how much God loves them."

When I ask how Central Coast Community Church avoids settling into a church routine after those 17 years, Wayne repeats the same line. "We exist for the people who aren't here yet—we are in a lower socioeconomic area in a borrowed hall that we have to set up every Friday night and pack up every Sabbath afternoon, so it keeps us feeling like we are in a mission field. That keeps us on edge."

INVOLVEMENT IS NOT OPTIONAL

Lessons from the front lines of urban mission

- **If you're a member, you're also a minister.** That's the credo that CCCC uses to foster member involvement in every aspect of the church's operations and ministries.
- **Look beyond internal dynamics.** Caring for the internal dynamics of the church is important, but it's not an end in itself. There's a reason for building a strong spiritual community—and that's to better reach the wider community for Christ.
- **A permanent church building isn't always necessary** for a growing, active church community. In fact, there can be definite mission advantages to not getting too "comfortable."
- **A long-term urban ministry requires a culture of leadership development**—a deliberate focus on giving individuals responsibility and training, early and often, starting even in the children's Sabbath Schools.

Find out more about Central Coast Community Church at www.cccc.org.au or www.facebook.com/cccchurch.

APPENDIX

In September 2013, Seventh-day Adventist leaders from around the world gathered at the General Conference world headquarters in Silver Spring, Maryland, for an urban mission conference called "It's Time." After five days of prayer, study, and discussion, they voted a series of recommendations to strengthen the urban influence of the Adventist Church, particularly in cities of more than 1 million people. The General Conference Executive Committee at Annual Council considered these recommendations and voted the following document in October 2013.

IT'S TIME

THE URGENCY OF URBAN MISSION

Where are we now?

The mission of the Seventh-day Adventist Church is to make disciples of Jesus Christ among all people, communicating the everlasting gospel in the context of the Three Angels' Messages of Revelation 14. And in many parts of the world Adventists have made significant advances toward that goal. However:

- For the first time in human history, more than half of the global population now lives in urban areas. By 2050 it is expected that 70 percent of the world will live in cities.

- There are more than 500 cities with a population of 1 million or more, 236 of which are in the 10/40 Window.

These 500 cities of 1 million or more:

- Have an average of one Adventist congregation for every 89,000 people.
- Include 100 cities where there is less than 1 Seventh-day Adventist for every 20,000 people.
- Include 45 cities with fewer than 10 Adventists.
- Include 43 cities without even 1 Adventist congregation.

These figures place a sobering challenge before the church, but they also should help us see the tremendous opportunities lying just before us.

Through the years, the church has given considerable attention to the work in cities and has often experienced God's blessing in establishing its presence there. But it is clear that the volume and pace of ministry in densely populated environments has not kept pace with the global movement towards urbanization. At times the size and complexity and the perceived negative influence of cities on spiritual life have made some people hesitant to fully engage in mission within cities.

And yet, we are continually reminded that Jesus said, "And this gospel of the kingdom will be preached in all the world as a witness to all the nations, and then the end will come" (Matthew 24:14, NKJV).

Ellen G. White wrote in 1912, "As the rays of the sun penetrate to the remotest corners of the globe, so God designs that the light of the gospel shall extend to every soul upon the earth. . . . His kingdom will not come until the good tidings of His grace shall have been carried to all the earth" (IHP 340 – RH Nov 14, 1912).

The cities of today are much larger and far more complex than those described in the Bible. However, God clearly loved the people of the cities—even those who were seen to be hostile to His people (see Jonah 4:11). On multiple occasions Jesus demonstrated compassion for the cities (Matthew 9:35–36). He wept over the city of Jerusalem (Luke 19:41). He ministered to people in a comprehensive manner, which dealt with the whole person—spiritual, social, physical, and mental (Matthew 4:23). The book of Acts in describing the spread of the gospel indicates that most, if not all, of the church planting efforts took place in cities (Acts 2:5, 8:5, 9:38, 11:19, etc.).

WHERE DO WE WANT TO BE?

In September/October 2013, church leaders from around the world met together for the *It's Time: Urban Mission Conference*. After several days of reviewing data, discussing ideas, and spending much time in prayer, these leaders adopted the following vision and goal for special emphasis through the next quinquennium:

THE VISION

That every city will have an influential Adventist presence actively engaged in a comprehensive mission, using Christ's method of ministry.

THE GOAL

To engage the collective resources of the global church in establishing a Seventh-day Adventist presence and needs-based ministry in cities of 1 million or more that have no Adventist congregation and, in all other cities of 1 million or more, to improve the ratio of members and worshipping groups to population.

And further, to ensure that divisions and their organizations, including local churches, give higher priority to the growing challenge of urban mission in their territory.

The church draws its inspiration for mission from the teaching and counsel of Jesus. It must also look to Him for its model of ministry—a comprehensive ministry that addressed the wide-ranging needs of the people around Him. Ellen White writes: "Christ's method alone will give true success in reaching the people. The Saviour mingled with men as one who desired their good. He showed His sympathy for them, ministered to their needs, and won their confidence. Then He bade them, 'Follow Me'" (*The Ministry of Healing*, p. 143).

Well over a century ago Ellen G. White appealed to church leadership to give special attention to the large cities of the world. "The work in the cities is the essential work for this time. When the cities are worked as God would have them, the result will be the setting in operation of a mighty movement such as we have not yet witnessed" (*Ministry to the Cities*, p. 10).

She wrote more about working in the cities than about leaving them. She comments that some members should move out but others should be carefully selected and sent into the cities to minister to the people. Major institutions should be established outside of the cities, but churches, primary schools, day care centers, restaurants, clinics, etc. should be located in the cities.

Some will live outside the city and work inside, others will need to live full-time in the city. Mrs. White recommends that outposts—places of physical and spiritual refreshing—should be provided for those living in the cities. These centers may include lifestyle health centers and training schools.[1]

It's time to refocus our attention on reaching out to the billions who live in the massive urban areas of the world.

HOW WILL WE GET THERE?

PROCESSES

In order to accomplish this goal, these resources and procedural steps have been identified:

1. That every division,[2] in consultation with its unions, conferences, and missions will accelerate and strengthen its current Mission to the Cities strategy by:

   a. Determining the comparative level of mission challenge among the cities of 1 million or more in their territories (by Annual Council, 2014).[3]

   b. Adopting initial time-based goals and mission implementation plans for cities of 1 million or more with no Adventist presence (by Annual Council, 2014).

   c. Adopting initial time-based goals and plans to improve the ratios of population to disciples and worshiping groups in cities of 1 million or more with an established Adventist presence (by Annual Council, 2014).

2. That General Conference, division, union, conference and mission administrations will have created and begun an effective communication strategy to inform

---

1 For further study, a new compilation of Ellen White's writings has been prepared by the White Estate. It is called *Ministry to the Cities*.

2 Whenever "division" is used it is understood to include MENA.

3 In areas where there are few or no cities of 1 million or more, plans may focus on smaller cities along with making plans to assist those areas of the world where there are many such cities.

and inspire the whole church for involvement in Mission to the Cities—its challenge, vision, and goals (by Annual Council, 2014).

3. That General Conference and division administrations will annually identify additional resources for use in cities that present the greatest level of urban mission challenge globally (by Annual Council each year, beginning in 2014).

4. That unions, conferences, and mission administrations will annually identify additional resources for use in cities that present the greatest level of urban mission challenge in their territories (beginning year-end meetings, 2014).

5. That the General Conference, in consultation with divisions, will help facilitate cross-division support and sponsorship for ministry in at least 100 of the most unentered cities of 1 million or more.

RESOURCES

The following resources have been identified as having special relevance for the work in the large urban areas of the world:

-   Spiritual: Ellen White says, "A revival of true godliness among us is the greatest and most urgent of all our needs. To seek this should be our first work" (1SM 121). Without the mighty power of the Holy Spirit the task is impossible (Zechariah 4:6). The immense challenge of reaching the cities calls for a united body of Christ to seek the power of the Holy Spirit through prayer, Bible study, and service.

-   Human resources: The Bible clearly calls every believer to a life of selfless serving, sacrificial giving, and active sharing of Christ's love. The apostle Paul instructs the early believers to use their spiritual gifts in faithful service as living witnesses. Every disciple of Jesus is called to be a partner in advancing His mission. The task of reaching the people of large urban areas will never be finished if we rely solely on pastors and professional evangelists.

- Financial Resources: Responding to the challenge of urban evangelism will require careful and prayerful prioritization of the church's resources. It also calls for sacrificial sharing of means by church entities and members.

Preparing people for comprehensive ministry in the cities will require careful attention to the following:

- Involving church members in planning for, and engaging in, urban mission and providing a supportive environment for their creative initiatives.

- Equipping church members to use their spiritual gifts in wholistic urban ministry, and helping to establish practical outlets for member-based ministry in every city through small groups, churches, and centers of influence.

- Carefully selecting and preparing people in urban areas to become involved with their community in avenues of needs-based ministry.

- Recruiting, training, and placing church planters to establish worshipping and witnessing groups in the least-reached people groups of each city.

- Encouraging each department and institution, at every level, to focus attention on processes, training, and resources for work in cities.

- Developing leaders for the church in the cities through academic and experienced-based programs with emphasis in cross-cultural training and understanding principles of sharing faith with those who come from other world religions.

Further, in order to stimulate urban mission everywhere each division is requested to encourage its field units and church membership to participate in a range of mission activity such as the following:

- Identifying and developing ways of reaching the least-reached people groups within each city

- Participating in community services
- Encouraging personal witnessing
- Embracing comprehensive health ministry
- Developing integrated media evangelism
- Empowering, equipping, and inspiring disciples for mission
- Establishing centers of influence
- Enhancing small group ministries
- Distributing literature
- Conducting public evangelism
- Developing relationships with public authorities.

HOW WILL WE KNOW WHAT IS BEING DONE?

Because the Bible encourages good stewardship and accountability, and in order to learn from experience, it is essential that our work in the cities has a careful plan of evaluation and accountability.

Such evaluation and accountability will be based on the shared goals defined above and will include:

1. A twice-yearly reporting and assessment system that informs the church about urban mission objectives, activities, and progress.

2. Regular quantitative and qualitative evaluations of goals and processes.

WHO IS RESPONSIBLE?

The responsibility for sharing the good news rests with all who are disciples of Jesus. Primary responsibility for planning, implementation, and evaluation rests with the leaders of the church at each level. The General Conference Office of Adventist Mission will assist the world church in this special focus on urban mission by coordinating with division leaders, General Conference departments and institutions.

HOW CAN I BE INVOLVED?

In order to reach the cities, the commitment and involvement of every member, church, and organization is needed.

Imagine the impact if millions of Seventh-day Adventists answered God's call to mission and if every church entity aligned itself with the goal to reach the billions in the cities around the world.

What if Seventh-day Adventists:
- Planted 10,000 new worship and ministry groups in cities of 1 million or more
- Initiated wholistic ministry in at least 100 of the most unentered cities of 1 million or more
- Established at least 5,000 centers of influence, including one in every city of 1 million or more
- Distributed 1 billion pieces of literature focused on urban areas
- Involved 2 million members in some form of health ministry in cities
- Involved Adventist churches in community service ministries in every city?

What if, in the 100 cities presenting the greatest mission challenge, the church:
- Placed 2,000 Global Mission pioneers
- Initiated ministry in the major media types and languages used
- Established early learning centers or primary schools
- Trained 2,000 people in the major languages of these cities
- Developed a plan to start or strengthen ADRA and church-based community service work
- Developed and maintained a database of at least 25,000 potential workers in order to respond to the rapidly changing opportunities that are developing in these cities
- Analyzed and reconfigured staffing requirements, at every administrative unit, to make available personnel and resources
- Encouraged and supported the development of creative new ministries?

As Seventh-day Adventists consider the world's vast cities, we are inspired by our Lord's passion for souls and by our pioneers' boldness in going "into all the world." We are moved by the billions of people living in large urban areas who have never heard of Jesus. We acknowledge that it is time that the Three Angels' Messages be proclaimed in all the big cities of the world. We dedicate ourselves to be active partners with Jesus Christ and His instruments for this immense task.

We recognize that this mission is challenging—but no more than the risk and challenge encountered by the apostles, the early church, and the Adventist pioneers.

We have a vital task to carry out, and we resolve to proclaim the message of the kingdom in every metropolis on earth—no matter the cost.

As church leaders, we commit ourselves to supporting the full use of the God-given talents of every church member in this pressing task, and we urge all Seventh-day Adventists to find ways to share Jesus in large urban areas. We encourage each member to ask God if He is calling him/her to minister in one of the great cities of the world. We ask church members and leaders at every level to prayerfully consider what they could do to support workers in large cities through prayer and giving.

The vision of a world that does not know Jesus compels us to make every possible sacrifice to cooperate with the mission of Jesus to reach His precious children in the cities.

"The great work of the gospel is not to close with less manifestation of the power of God than marked its opening," writes Ellen White. "The prophecies which were fulfilled in the outpouring of the former rain at the opening of the gospel are again to be fulfilled in the latter rain at its close" (*The Great Controversy*, p. 611).

Our Lord's commission in Matthew 24 and John's prophetic vision in Revelation 14 are the heartbeat and hope of Seventh-day Adventists, and they urgently call us to recognize—*It's time!*